Ace Your Case® VI
Mastering the Case Interview

WetFeet Insider Guide

WetFeet, Inc.
The Folger Building
101 Howard Street
Suite 300
San Francisco, CA 94105

Phone: (415) 284-7900 or 1-800-926-4JOB
Fax: (415) 284-7910
Website: www.WetFeet.com

Ace Your Case® VI: Mastering the Case Interview
ISBN: 1-58207-538-7

Photocopying Is Prohibited

Copyright 2005 WetFeet, Inc. All rights reserved. This publication is protected by the copyright laws of the United States of America. No copying in any form is permitted. It may not be reproduced, distributed, stored in a retrieval system, or transmitted in any form or by any means, in part or in whole, without the express written permission of WetFeet, Inc.

The publisher, author, and any other party involved in creation, production, delivery, or sale of this WetFeet Insider Guide make no warranty, express or implied, about the accuracy or reliability of the information found herein. To the degree you use this guide or other materials referenced herein, you do so at your own risk. The materials contained herein are general in nature and may not apply to particular factual or legal circumstances. Under no circumstances shall the publisher, author, or any other party involved in creation, production or delivery of this guide be liable to you or any other person for damages of any kind arising from access to, or use of, its content.

Table of Contents

Ace Your Case VI at a Glance 1

The Interview Unplugged 3
Overview 4
The Case Interview 6

Case-by-Case Rules 13
Market-Sizing Cases 14
Business Operations Cases 17
Business Strategy Cases 20
Resume Cases 22

The Practice Range 25
Market-Sizing Case Questions 26
Business Operations Case Questions 31
Business Strategy Case Questions 38
Resume Case Questions 47

TABLE OF CONTENTS

Nailing the Case 53
Market-Sizing Case Questions 55
Business Operations Case Questions 78
Business Strategy Case Questions. 99
Resume Case Questions 124

Ace Your Case VI at a Glance

Here's a summary of the different types of cases you'll find in this report, along with some rules that should help you ace your answer.

Market-Sizing Questions

- Use round numbers.
- Show your work.
- Use paper and calculator.

Business Operations Questions

- Isolate the main issue.
- Apply a framework.
- Think action!

Business Strategy Questions

- Think frameworks.
- Ask questions.
- Work from big to small.

Resume Cases

- Know your story.
- Keep the *Parent Test* in mind.
- Let your excitement shine!

ACE YOUR CASE® VI

The Interview Unplugged

Overview

The Case Interview

Overview

When it comes to preparing for your case interviews, there's one word and one word only: practice. By now, you're spending all of your spare time thinking about why Google is getting into e-mail, why customer service jobs are moving to India, and how much mustard is consumed in Idaho. Your family thinks you're an oddball, but you're on the right track. You're probably even starting to enjoy thinking about these issues. Watch out: You might be turning into a consultant.

This guide is designed to be a companion volume to *Ace Your Case!*, *Ace Your Case II*, *Ace Your Case III*, *Ace Your Case IV*, and *Ace Your Case V*. It offers a brand new set of case questions and answers accompanied by new detailed explanations about the different case types. Many of our sample case questions are based on real, live case questions that people received in their interviews last year.

For those who haven't seen our other case-interviewing guides, *Ace Your Case!* discusses the consulting interview in general and offers a primer containing a number of common frameworks and B-school–type tools (watch out for the 4Cs and the 4Ps, not to mention the infamous Five Forces) that should help you attack your case questions. *Ace Your Case II*, *Ace Your Case III*, *Ace Your Case IV*, and *Ace Your Case V* each contain 15 specific case questions and detailed recommended answers, as does this edition.

A word about how to use this guide: We strongly recommend that you try to solve the questions first, without looking at the answers. After you've given them your best shot, go ahead and check out our recommended answers. If you find that our "good answer" differs from yours, see whether there's something you can learn from our suggestions. But don't panic—there are usually numerous ways to answer any case question. It's far more important to note the approach, as well as the interviewer's likely responses, which obviously won't be included in your own answers. As you sharpen those skills, keep thinking to yourself, "I love these case questions!" Pretty soon you'll find yourself talking like a consultant!

 **INSIDER TIP**

Keep the firm's reputation and areas of strength in mind as you launch into your case answer. Firms that are known for a particular type of work are likely to be more sensitive to those issues in the case questions they give.

The Case Interview

BACKGROUND

Many management consulting firms, especially the strategy firms (McKinsey, Boston Consulting Group, Bain, Mercer, et al.) love to give prospective employees a problem to solve during the course of the interview. These problem-solving exercises, known generally as "case questions," are designed to help the interviewer screen candidates and determine which people really have what it takes to be a real, live, card-carrying management consultant.

Case questions come in many forms and levels of complexity. To help you get a handle on them, we have identified four different categories of questions:

- Market-sizing questions
- Business operations questions
- Business strategy questions
- Resume questions

(Note that we are not covering the brainteaser category in this Insider Guide. Consulting firms rarely ask brainteaser questions; other types of cases give much more insight into the type of thinking that makes a good consultant.)

Each of these prototypes has certain distinguishing features, which we discuss below. In addition, our insiders recommend certain "rules of the road" that should help you successfully navigate the different types of questions. Don't worry—you'll never be asked to spit out a category name and serial number for the questions you receive in the interview. Nevertheless, if you can identify the type of question, you will have a better idea about how to effectively attack the problem.

WHAT YOUR INTERVIEWER IS SEEKING

It may seem as if your interviewer is using the case technique for one purpose alone: to humiliate prospective consultants. Although a few interviewers do seem to take a perverse pleasure in watching candidates writhe, this isn't the true goal of the technique. According to insiders, case questions really do help interviewers evaluate a candidate's aptitude for consulting. What does that mean exactly? Whether you're an undergrad, an MBA, or a PhD, consulting interviewers will likely depend on the case questions to check you out on the following dimensions:

- Analytical ability
- Structured thinking
- Intelligence
- Ability to not break into hives under pressure
- Common sense
- Ability to think on your feet
- Interest in problem solving
- Business intuition
- Facility with numbers
- Presentation skills
- Communication skills
- Ability to sort through information and focus on the key points
- Ability to analyze and then make recommendations based on the analysis
- Creativity
- Enthusiasm

Before you bid all your points to get an interview with name-your-consulting-firm, we recommend that you spend some time thinking about how consulting fits you. In particular, you must have good answers to two questions:

- Why do you want to be a consultant?
- And why do you want to work for this firm?

If you have good answers to these two questions, then you're ready to start thinking about cases. We start by discussing the case interview as it relates to several categories of candidates: undergraduates, MBAs, advanced-degree candidates, and experienced hires.

UNDERGRADUATES

Consulting interviewers tell us that the case questions and the expected answers for undergraduates tend to be simpler and more understandable than those for MBA students. Market-sizing questions are very popular (you will almost certainly get at least one of these), as are general business strategy problems. In the business strategy area, the companies and the topics may also seem a little friendlier; you're more likely to get a case about a beer company than about a company trying to license the latest packet-filtering technology for data encryption. Operations questions (with the exception of the ever-popular declining-profits question) are less common for undergraduates, and resume questions will more likely focus on academic or extracurricular activities than on work experiences.

Interviewers say that they often provide more prompting to undergraduate candidates during the interview. In evaluating your answer to a question, only the most sadistic interviewer would expect you to regurgitate all of the standard business-school terminology and techniques (after all, how else could the company justify paying MBAs the big bucks?). But beware: Rank amateurs are definitely not welcome. Thus, you must have a general understanding of basic business relationships (e.g., revenues − costs = profits), but don't get your knickers in a knot if you can't name even one of the Five Forces.

Here are a few real, live case questions fielded by our undergraduate customers:

- How many kitchens are installed in the United States each year?
- Your client is thinking about expanding her sourcing operations into China. What are some of the issues she should think about?
- Your client is a manufacturer of high-end, branded watches. Prices are falling dramatically in the category. What should your client do?

MBAS

MBAs have long been the heavy hitters of the consulting workforce. As a result, the case interview reaches its most sophisticated and demanding form in the MBA interview. All types of questions—from the simple market-sizer to the gnarliest of business strategy problems—are fair game. Practically any industry or functional issue area is possible material for the case question. An MBA candidate will be expected to be familiar with a number of the standard MBA frameworks and concepts. Also, the case will possibly have a few tricky twists or turns. For example, what might seem like a pure and simple international strategy question might be complicated by an unexpected restriction related to the European regulatory environment.

Interviewers tell us that most MBAs have a polished interview technique and understand the basics of many case problems. Therefore, they look for depth in the answer (what they describe as an ability to peel the onion and a real familiarity with business concepts). We understand that at least some recruiters like to ask resume case questions because they provide an opportunity to get more detail about the candidate's background and problem-solving experiences.

Here are a few real, live case questions fielded by our MBA customers:

- How many pieces of mail are delivered to houses in the United States in a year?
- Your client has 200 physical therapy locations and is seeking to expand into chiropractics. Should he do it?
- Should your client, a major commercial real estate development company, expand into residential real estate?

OTHER ADVANCED-DEGREE CANDIDATES

Although consulting firms attract mostly MBA applicants, several of the top firms have started to look beyond traditional feeder programs to identify top talent. According to WetFeet customers and recruiters, the different firms have very different approaches to advanced-degree candidates. McKinsey and BCG, among others, have recruiting programs aimed at PhDs, MDs, JDs, and others at the top schools. In the process, some of these firms have created customized recruiting and training programs for advanced-degree candidates. Other firms continue to consider advanced-degree candidates on a case-by-case basis, often pitting them against undergraduate or MBA candidates, depending on their background.

If you enter a separate recruiting track, you will, according to our customers, still have to contend with interviews that are similar in format to that of undergraduate and MBA recruiting programs. In other words, expect a heavy dose of case interview questions along with the general get-to-know-you queries. One slight difference is that, in addition to seeing whether you can handle the substance of the case question, the recruiter will also be looking to see "if [you] can break out of the PhD box." In other words, can you adapt to the real world and answer questions without giving too much detail?

According to WetFeet customers, case questions for advanced-degree candidates usually don't require you to carry your own MBA toolbox. Instead, the questions may relate to previous research (your resume is usually a font of material), or they may resemble undergraduate case studies that check a person's intuition, common sense, analytical skills, and problem-solving abilities. Interviewers at various top firms say they may be more inclined to prompt advance-degree candidates with questions, and they may be satisfied with a good, solid, analytical answer that doesn't necessarily incorporate all of the latest business buzzwords.

Check out these case questions fielded by our advanced-degree customers:

- How many turkeys are consumed on Thanksgiving?

- Your client has come across a major innovation, but has determined it does not currently have the capabilities to sell it profitably. Should it "buy" the capabilities, "build" them internally, or license the innovation?

- Question for someone in life sciences: What do you think the impact of genomics will be on large pharmaceutical companies?

EXPERIENCED HIRES

If you are seeking to join a consulting firm from industry or from another consulting firm, your interviewing experience may differ from that described in this report. According to WetFeet customers, experienced-hire candidates may or may not face a battery of case questions. There is no hard-and-fast rule, but it seems as though people with more experience (10-plus years) and people who have already worked for a name-brand consulting firm are relatively unlikely to face a case as part of their review process. In contrast, people who have worked in industry for a few years and who are seeking to enter consulting at a middle level are likely to go through a process similar to that used for MBAs (i.e., expect lots of cases). In particular, if you are changing careers (e.g., moving from nonprofit work to consulting) and not signing on as an industry authority, you'll probably be scrutinized for your consulting aptitude—as demonstrated by your ability to field case questions.

Typical case questions faced by our experienced-hire customers include:

- A young entrepreneur has hired you to help her market a new product that will transform home entertainment. Through which channels would you recommend she market her innovation?

- Your client is Yosemite Park. Park revenues have declined significantly over the last few years. How could Yosemite boost revenues?

- Specific questions related to their area of expertise.

COMPANY-SPECIFIC VARIATIONS

As you enter the ring with consultants from a variety of firms, you'll probably notice differences in the questions you receive, as well as the style and approach of the case interview. More often than not, these differences arise from the differences in the personalities and experiences of your interviewers. However, several firms have developed their own approach to the case interview. One variation involves giving a candidate a written case before the interview and asking him to prepare to discuss the case in detail during the interview. We understand that IBM Global Services (formerly PricewaterhouseCoopers) and Monitor Group have given preprinted cases to candidates before an interview. Monitor has also used a group interview technique that requires competing candidates to work with each other to solve a problem, while McKinsey has experimented with a process for undergraduates that includes both a written case test and a group interview.

One other thing to keep in mind: Recruiters suggest that you would be wise to keep the firm's reputation and areas of strength in mind as you launch into your case answer. Firms that are known for a particular type of work are likely to be more sensitive to those issues in the case questions they give. For example, if you're interviewing with Towers Perrin, you shouldn't be surprised to find a people issue somewhere in the case. If you're talking with Deloitte Consulting, keep operations in mind as you craft an answer—and don't talk about how it's important to work only with the company's top management. And, if you're interviewing with Bain, remember how much importance the company attaches to measurable results and data-driven analysis.

Case-by-Case Rules

Market-Sizing Cases

Business Operations Cases

Business Strategy Cases

Resume Cases

Market-Sizing Cases

OVERVIEW

Consultants love to ask market-sizing questions. Not only are they easy to create, discuss, and evaluate, they are also highly representative of an important type of work done by consultants. In their simplest form, market-sizing cases require the candidate to determine the size of a particular market (hence the name). In the real world, this information can be especially helpful when gauging the attractiveness of a new market. In the interview context, a market-sizing question might be pitched in an extremely straightforward manner (e.g., "What is the market for surfboards in the United States?"). Or it may be disguised as a more complex question (e.g., "Do you think Fidelity should come out with a mutual fund targeted at high-net-worth individuals?") that requires the respondent to peel away the extraneous detail to identify the market-sizing issue at the core. In a more highly developed variation, the interviewer might ask a strategy or operations case question that requires the respondent to do some market-sizing in order to come up with an appropriate recommendation.

THE SCORECARD

Market-sizing questions allow the interviewer to test the candidate's facility with numbers, powers of analysis, and common sense. For example, if you were asked to size the surfboard market, you would need to make basic assumptions about the market. (How many people surf? How many boards does a typical surfer dude or gal own? How often will he or she get a new one? Are there other big purchasers besides individual surfers? Is there a market for used boards?) You would also need to make a few basic calculations (number of surfers x number of new boards per year + total quantity purchased by other types of customers, etc.). As you work through these issues, the interviewer would also get a glimpse of your common sense. (Did you assume that everybody in the U.S. population would be a potential surfer, or did you try to estimate the population in prime surfing areas like California and Hawaii?)

> **We get the 'deer in the headlights' look from time to time. That's an automatic ding.**

LOCATION

Market-sizing questions can pop up in all interviews. They are almost certain to make an appearance in undergraduate and advanced-degree interviews. Indeed, both undergraduates and PhDs report receiving exactly the same market-sizing questions in their respective interviews. MBAs are also likely to receive market-sizing questions; however, a common and more complex variation typical of an MBA interview involves assessing the opportunity for a new product. For example, you might be asked whether your pharmaceutical company client should develop and market a drug for male pattern baldness. Part of the analysis would require you to estimate the market potential (i.e., market size) for the drug.

MASTERING YOUR MARKET-SIZING QUESTIONS

Market-sizing questions can intimidate. But once you understand the rules (and practice your technique), you can come to view these cases as slow pitches right over the center of the plate. So, just how many golf balls are used in the United States in a year? You don't know, and the truth is, neither does your interviewer. In fact, your interviewer doesn't even care what the real number is. But remember, she does care about your ability to use logic, common sense, and creativity to get to a plausible answer. And she wants to make sure you don't turn tail when you've got a few numbers to run. Which brings us to the three rules for market-sizing questions.

Rule 1: Use Round Numbers

Even if you weren't a multivariate calculus stud, you can impress your interviewer with your number-crunching abilities if you stick to round numbers. They're much easier to add, subtract, multiply, and divide, and since we've already decided that the exact answer doesn't matter anyway, go ahead and pick something that you can toss around with ease. Good examples? One hundred, one million, ten dollars, two, one-half. The population of New York City? Ten million, give or take. The length of a standard piece of paper? Round 11 inches up to a foot.

Rule 2: Show Your Work

Case questions are the ultimate "show your work" questions. In fact, your exact answer matters less than the path you took to get there. Remember, the market-sizing question is merely a platform through which your interviewer can test your analysis, creativity, and comfort with numbers.

Rule 3: Use Paper and Calculator

If you feel more comfortable writing everything down and using a calculator, do! Most interviewers will not care if you use a pencil and paper to keep your thoughts organized and logical. And if pulling out the HP to multiply a few numbers keeps you from freaking out, then by all means do it. Your interviewer will be more impressed if you are calm, cool, and collected, so if using props helps you, then go for it.

Business Operations Cases

OVERVIEW

A fair number of case questions cover operations issues. Given the existing economic environment, the mix of consulting business has shifted more toward operations and process-focused cases, so be prepared for at least one of these types of questions. Broadly speaking, operations refers to everything that's involved in running a business and getting product out the door. In a manufacturing plant, this would include the purchasing and transporting of raw materials, the manufacturing processes, the scheduling of staff and facilities, the distribution of the product, the servicing of equipment in the field, and so on. In its broadest sense, operations would even include the sales and marketing of the company's products and the systems used to track sales. Whereas strategy questions deal with the future direction of the firm (e.g., whether to enter a new line of business), operations deals with the day-to-day running of the business. It is particularly fertile ground for consulting work, and for case questions. Some of the most typical case questions of this type are those that require the candidate to explain why a company's sales or profits have declined.

THE SCORECARD

Consultants like to ask operations questions because they allow the interviewer to see whether the candidate understands fundamental issues related to running a business (e.g., the relationship between revenues and costs, and the relationship and impact of fixed costs and variable costs on a company's profitability). In addition, operations questions require the candidate to demonstrate a good grasp of process and an ability to sort through a pile of information and identify the most important factors.

LOCATION

Operations questions are fair game for all candidates, including undergraduates and advanced-degree candidates. According to our customers, the declining profits questions are some of the most popular types of cases around, and almost all candidates can expect to get at least one of these. That said, MBAs are typically expected to explore these questions in greater detail and have a better grasp of key business issues and terminology. MBAs could also get tossed more complicated operations questions. For example, an MBA case might involve understanding the implications of allocating fixed costs in a certain way, or, perhaps, the impact on the balance sheet of a certain type of financing.

Undergraduates and non-MBA candidates still need to be familiar with a few basic operational concepts, such as the relationship between costs and revenues, and the various things that might have an impact on them. In addition, undergraduates might expect the topic of the question to be more familiar. For example, an undergraduate might get lobbed a question about the implications of launching a new national chain of restaurants. An MBA might get a question about factors that would allow a manufacturing operation to increase throughput.

OPTIMIZING YOUR BUSINESS OPERATIONS ANSWERS

Operations case questions are more complex than market-sizing questions. Not only do they typically require basic business knowledge (or, at the very least, a good deal of common sense), but they also frequently require the candidate to think like a detective. For example, the interviewer might ask why an airline has been losing money while its market share has increased. There could be many reasons for this: Revenues might be down (and that, in turn, might be caused by any number of things, including ticket price wars, lower ridership, growing accounts payable, and so on); costs might be higher (due to higher fuel costs, greater landing fees, higher plane maintenance costs, and other factors); or the airline could be operating more inefficiently (e.g., higher passenger loads might require it to lease additional aircraft or pay staff overtime). In any case, a successful analysis of the question requires the candidate to think clearly and efficiently about the question. To help with these types of questions, here are some rules you'll want to keep in mind.

Rule 1: Isolate the Main Issue

Operations questions usually have lots of potential answers. The first step in identifying a good answer (and demonstrating your analytical firepower) is to separate the wheat from the chaff. Once you've zeroed in on the main issue, you'll be able to apply your energy to working out a good conclusion to the problem.

Rule 2: Apply a Framework

Frameworks were made for cracking operations questions. They will help you sift through lots of data and organize your answer. A useful framework can be something as simple as saying, "If the airline is losing money, it has something to do with either costs or revenues," and moving on to talk about each of these areas in turn.

Rule 3: Think Action!

Unlike your market-sizing question, operations questions never end with a nice, neat analysis. Rather, the goal here is action. The hypothetical client is usually facing a critical issue: Revenues are falling, costs are rising, production is crashing. Something needs to be done. As a consultant, you will be hired to give advice. As a candidate, you should be sensitive to the fact that your analysis must drive toward a solution. Even if you need more data before you're able to make a final recommendation, you should acknowledge that you are evaluating various courses of action. Better yet, you should lay out a plan for next steps.

Business Strategy Cases

OVERVIEW

Business strategy cases are the granddaddies (and demons) of the case question world. Consultants love to use these questions because they touch on so many different issues. A good strategy question can have a market-sizing piece, a logic puzzle, multiple operations issues, and a major dose of creativity and action thrown in for good measure. Moreover, a complex strategy question can go in many different directions, thereby allowing the interviewer to probe the candidate's abilities in a variety of areas. Again, strategy case questions can run the gamut from a complex, multi-industry, multinational, multi-issue behemoth to a localized question with a pinpoint focus.

THE SCORECARD

Depending on the nature of the question, the interviewer can use it to assess anything and everything from your ability to handle numbers to your ability to wade through a mass of detailed information and synthesize it into a compelling business strategy. Of all the different types of case questions, these are also the most similar to the actual work you'll do on the job (at least at the strategy firms). One other thing the interviewer will be checking carefully: your presentation skills.

LOCATION

Strategy case questions are fair game for any type of candidate. For undergraduates, they will often be more two-dimensional and straightforward. For MBA candidates, they frequently have several layers of issues, and perhaps an international or other twist to boot. Although most strategy boutiques will use this kind of case as a mainstay in their recruiting efforts, firms with more of an operations focus may rely more heavily on operations questions.

SIMPLIFYING THE STRATEGY STUMPERS

Because business strategy questions can involve many different elements, they may inspire fear in the weak of heart. Although it's true that strategy questions can be the most difficult, they can also be the most fun. This is your opportunity to play CEO, or at least advisor to the CEO. You can put all of your business intuition and your hard-nosed, data-driven research to work and come up with a plan that will bring a huge multinational corporation into the limelight—or not. Does it matter that you just crafted a story about why a credit card company should go into the Italian market when your best friend who interviewed immediately prior to you recommended against going Italian? No, not really. Unless, of course, your friend did a better job of exploring the case question. What does that mean? By going through this book (and the other WetFeet *Ace Your Case* guides), you're already a step ahead of the game. However, here are the rules you'll want to keep in mind as you tackle your strategy case questions.

Rule 1: Think Frameworks

While analyzing a really juicy strategy question, you might be able to draw information and jargon out of almost every course in your school's core business curriculum. Don't succumb to temptation! Your interviewer will be much more impressed by a clear and simple story about how you are attacking the question and where you are going with your analysis. The best way to do this is to apply a framework to the problem. As with operations questions, this means setting out a plan of attack up front and following it through to conclusion. One other big benefit: Having a clear framework will help you organize your analysis.

Rule 2: Ask Questions

Successful consulting is as much about asking the right questions as it is about providing a good answer. Likewise, your solution to a strategy case will be much better if you've focused your energy on the right issue. To help you get there, don't hesitate to ask your interviewer questions. In the best case, he may help you avoid a derailment; in the worst case, he'll understand your thought process as you plow through the analysis.

Rule 3: Work from Big to Small

Even though the strategy case you are examining was the subject of a study that lasted several months, you probably have about 15 minutes to provide your answer. Therefore it's essential that you start by looking at the most significant issues first. Besides, this is a great discipline for future consultants; the client may be paying for your time by the hour, so you'll want to make sure that you really are adding value.

Resume Cases

OVERVIEW

One favorite type of alternative case question is the resume case. Instead of cooking up a case question based on a carefully disguised project from his files, the interviewer will pull something straight from the candidate's resume. Usually, these cases stem from a previous professional experience, but occasionally you'll get something like: "I see you play rugby. Describe for me all of the different positions on a rugby team, and the play strategy for each." Frequently, the interviewer will ask the candidate to walk through a previous work project or experience and explain how he or she decided on a particular course of action. As the candidate goes through the discussion, the interviewer may then change a few critical assumptions and ask the candidate to explain how he would have responded. For example, if you had started and run a successful computer repair service, the interviewer might ask how you would have responded if a local computer store had created a knock-off service and offered it at a lower price.

THE SCORECARD

The resume case is a way for the interviewer to dig a little deeper into your resume and at the same time test your case-cracking capabilities. (It also adds a little variety to a grueling day of interviews.) Here, the interviewer is testing for your ability to communicate—in layman's terms—a topic that is very familiar to you. Resume cases are generally a good opportunity for you to toot your own horn a bit about your past experience and exude confidence, competence, and enthusiasm about things you really understand.

LOCATION

The resume question is fair game for undergrads, MBAs, and advanced-degree candidates. Naturally, because the resumes for each type of candidate differ significantly, the types of questions also differ. MBAs can expect business-oriented questions; advanced-degree candidates can expect questions related to their previous research. PhD students tell us that they commonly receive resume cases. Not only do resume cases allow the candidate to avoid feeling like she has to master a whole new lexicon and body of frameworks, they test her communications skills.

ROCKING YOUR RESUME CASES

Because the resume case question takes the discussion to your home turf, there isn't really a secret recipe for pulling apart the question. Rather, the way to be successful here is to follow a few basic interview rules.

Rule 1: Know Your Story

Nothing will make you look worse—and help you find the door more quickly—than not knowing what you put on your own resume. Make sure you've reviewed all of the items on your resume before the interview. Write down a few notes about what you did at each job, and the main message you want to convey through each bullet point on your resume. Think up a short story for each bullet point that will provide compelling evidence to support those messages.

Rule 2: Keep the *Parent Test* in Mind

This is not the place to play the polyglot; nobody will be impressed with your ability to speak techno-babble. The interviewer will assume that you know everything there is to know about your area of expertise, whether that's molecular biology or your computer-repair service. The real question is can you tell others about what you did without sending them into a coma? It may sound easy, but many people seem incapable of communicating what they know. Our suggestion? Practice talking about your work as if you were telling your parents all about it.

Rule 3: Let Your Excitement Shine

This is your home field, so use it to your advantage. Talk about your past work with energy and enthusiasm. Believe it or not, even consultants like a little passion. Besides, if you're sitting there griping about a previous work experience, guess what's running through your interviewer's mind: "Whoa, Nelly. This cat could be trouble!"

The Practice Range

Market-Sizing Case Questions

Business Operations Case Questions

Business Strategy Case Questions

Resume Case Questions

Market-Sizing Case Questions

Remember the rules for market-sizing questions:

1. Use round numbers.//
2. Show your work.
3. Use paper and calculator.

ACE YOUR CASE® VI

THE PRACTICE RANGE

 **CASE 1**

How many pieces of luggage fly through the San Francisco airport in a 24-hour period?

Key questions to ask:

_____

_____

_____

_____

Basic equations/numbers:

_____

_____

_____

_____

How you'd track the numbers down:

_____

_____

_____

_____

CASE 2

How many new golf balls are sold each year? Only consider golf balls sold to individuals (e.g. exclude golf balls sold at ranges).

Key questions to ask:

Basic equations/numbers:

How you'd track the numbers down:

 **CASE 3**

It's a hot summer weekend day. How many movie tickets are purchased at the local theater?

Key questions to ask:

Basic equations/numbers:

How you'd track the numbers down:

CASE 4

How many pounds of potatoes does McDonald's buy each week to support its U.S. operations?

Key questions to ask:

___

Basic equations/numbers:

___

How you'd track the numbers down:

___

ACE YOUR CASE® VI

THE PRACTICE RANGE

Business Operations Case Questions

Remember the rules for business operations questions:

1. Isolate the main issue.

2. Apply a framework.

3. Think action!

CASE 5

The president of a large pencil and pen company has hired your consulting firm to assess why profits have fallen from respectable levels 4 years ago to a net loss this year. You have been assigned the role of main business analyst on the engagement. You have enough information to know that the client has some kind of operations issue at play that has increased expenses and eroded profitability—but no one knows what the issue is. How would you go about analyzing the situation and assessing the source(s) of this company's operations problem?

Key questions to ask:

_____

_____

_____

_____

_____

What are the main issues?

_____

_____

_____

_____

_____

CASE 5

Key approaches/frameworks:

Possible courses of action:

CASE 6

The managing partner of one of the larger regional offices of a management consulting company is concerned because he has noticed an industry-wide reduction in consulting spending during the previous year. He is thinking about the impact this might have on how he runs his management consulting practice within his own office, and he has asked for your help in thinking about it. What would you like to know, and how would you advise this managing partner to react to his situation?

Key questions to ask:

_____

_____

_____

_____

_____

What are the main issues?

_____

_____

_____

_____

_____

CASE 6

Key approaches/frameworks:

_____

_____

_____

_____

_____

_____

Possible courses of action:

_____

_____

_____

_____

_____

_____

_____

_____

_____

 CASE 7

The CEO of Bon Jeans, a famous jeans producer, has come to you for help with his retail division. His company sold jeans primarily through department stores until 2 years ago. Once that channel became saturated, the company decided to launch retail stores to capture additional sales. The stores got off to a flying start, but have recently been declining in profitability—to the point that the company's retail division has become unprofitable. What's making the stores unprofitable?

Key questions to ask:

What are the main issues?

ACE YOUR CASE® VI

THE PRACTICE RANGE

CASE 7

Key approaches/frameworks:

Possible courses of action:

Business Strategy Case Questions

Keep the rules for business strategy questions in mind:

1. Think frameworks.

2. Ask questions.

3. Work from small to big.

ACE YOUR CASE® VI

THE PRACTICE RANGE

 **CASE 8**

Your client is an operator of 20 restaurants in a medium-sized metropolitan city. Currently, it serves only lunch and dinner. It is thinking of expanding its offerings to include breakfast as well. What would you advise your client to do?

Key questions to ask:

What are the main issues?

CASE 8 (CONT'D)

Key approaches/frameworks:

_____

_____

_____

_____

_____

Outline for my answer:

_____

_____

_____

_____

_____

Action recommendations:

_____

_____

_____

_____

_____

 **CASE 9**

You have just been hired by Pluto, a candy company with a long tradition of making chocolaty treats. You have joined a 6-month old division that has been tasked with diversifying the company's product offerings by developing a new candy product that is not chocolate-based. You have been hired as a business analyst reporting to the lead product manager on this new product—but the exact product has not yet been conceived, named, or launched. What would you want to know in order to supply your team with the right information to determine what product your new division should make? How would you get that information?

Key questions to ask:

What are the main issues?

CASE 9 (CONT'D)

Key approaches/frameworks:

_____
_____
_____
_____
_____

Outline for my answer:

_____
_____
_____
_____
_____

Action recommendations:

_____
_____
_____
_____
_____
_____

ACE YOUR CASE® VI

THE PRACTICE RANGE

 **CASE 10**

Your client is a major pharmaceutical company whose research and development department has developed a promising new drug compound, but is uncertain as to what to do with it. Should it license its brand or manage the entry in-house?

Key questions to ask:

What are the main issues?

CASE 10 (CONT'D)

Key approaches/frameworks:

___

Outline for my answer:

___

Action recommendations:

___

CASE 11

Your client is the vice president of marketing for a major cosmetic company. He is considering whether or not to introduce a line of men's cologne for Wal-Mart. What are the major issues he should be thinking about?

Key questions to ask:

What are the main issues?

CASE 11 (CONT'D)

Key approaches/frameworks:

_____

_____

_____

_____

_____

Outline for my answer:

_____

_____

_____

_____

_____

Action recommendations:

_____

_____

_____

_____

_____

Resume Case Questions

Remember the rules for resume questions:

1. Know your story.
2. Keep the *Parent Test* in mind.
3. Let your excitement shine!

CASE 12

Talk to me about a business leader for whom you have a lot of respect.

CASE 13

Tell me about a business trend that you're following closely.

CASE 14

What other industries are you considering entering? Why is consulting your first choice?

 **CASE 15**

Objectively, as if you were answering on behalf of a colleague or supervisor at your former employer, tell me what you consider to be your biggest opportunity for development and improvement—the weak spot in your skill set as compared to your strengths.

Nailing the Case

Market-Sizing Case Questions

Business Operations Case Questions

Business Strategy Case Questions

Resume Case Questions

INSIDER TIP

The destination is often less important to your interviewer than the road you take to get there.

Now it's time to walk through sample answers to each of the questions posed in "The Practice Range." Although we believe that our recommended answers are good, we know that there are many equally good and even better answers out there. Remember, the destination is often less important to your interviewer than the road you take to get there. With that in mind, smooth sailing! A quick note on the layout: Each question is followed by bad answers (which are admittedly a bit far-fetched in some cases) and a good answer. The questions and dialogue between the hypothetical recruiter and candidate appear in normal type; the WetFeet analysis and commentary appear in italics.

Market-Sizing Case Questions

CASE 1

How many pieces of luggage fly through the San Francisco airport in a 24-hour period?

This is a straightforward question suitable for either an undergraduate or an advance-degree candidate.

Bad Answers

- Gosh, I have never been to the San Francisco airport before. Could you ask me a different question instead?

It is never a good idea to tell the interviewer that you cannot answer a question. She is interested in how you would structure the problem, not the specific answer that you reach—the name of the airport in the question is not important. It might even be helpful to think about a familiar airport first to get to an approach.

- I read in the *Wall Street Journal* yesterday that San Francisco airport is the fourth busiest airport in the country with 50,000 passengers a day. Everybody is allowed two bags, so that is 100,000 bags a day.

This answer is too quick and involves little thought. The interviewer will not be impressed by the fact that you remember some little known fact from the WSJ. He is more interested in understanding how you think through problems. The candidate has not considered all of the key factors that impact how many bags different segments of air travelers might bring—international vs domestic flights or business vs leisure travelers.

Good Answer

Candidate: That is an interesting question, with a number of different dimensions to it. If you think about it, there are a number of different types of luggage that could be going through the airport: freight, personal luggage, unaccompanied baggage, etc. Also, different types of people need different amounts of luggage. There are even questions around what day of the week we are looking at, and the time of year, too.

Always take a few moments to think before starting to answer any case question. Plan out an approach before you start speaking. In this case the candidate has made a good start to answering the question. He has identified some of the main drivers that will affect the outcome of the market-sizing effort, showing the interviewer that he is on the ball.

Candidate: I think the best way to approach this is to start by defining what we are going to include in our definition of luggage. As I just mentioned, there are different types of luggage flying everyday. Can we assume that we are just talking about personal luggage—luggage taken by airline passengers traveling to or from San Francisco, both carry-on and checked luggage?

Defining and agreeing to parameters not only helps the candidate to more concisely structure the problem, it also ensures that the candidate and the interviewer are on the same page and are expecting to address the same problem.

Interviewer: That sounds like a reasonable assumption to make. Let's assume that we are only talking about passengers' luggage and not cargo.

Candidate: Great, just one more clarifying point before I move on. For the moment, can I assume that we are talking about an average 24-hour period, i.e., not the day before a big holiday, etc.? This will obviously have a big impact on the number of people traveling.

It is always better to clarify your assumptions out loud for the interviewer. Do not put the interviewer in a position where she has to make assumptions about what you are thinking. She may not always realize you made the assumption and simply think you forgot to consider an important point—in this case holiday traffic.

Interviewer: Yes, that sounds fine. Let's assume that we are talking about an average Tuesday for the moment. So, what do you think?

Candidate: Okay, so to answer this question I really need two pieces of data. First, I need to know how many pieces of luggage the average passenger carries. Second, I need to know how many passengers are traveling through the airport in a 24-hour period.

It is important to outline any structure or process you are going to apply to the problem up front so that the interviewer understands where you will be leading her and how you expect to get to the answer.

Candidate: Let's start by thinking about how many pieces of luggage the average passenger carries. It is quite difficult to estimate this, as there are so many different types of passengers out there, each with different luggage needs. I mean there is the business guy who just takes a carry-on for his 2-day trip, and then you have the family going on vacation with the legal limit of both carry-on and checked luggage. So, I think that we should split the passengers into two broad groups: business travelers and leisure travelers.

The candidate has realized that not all passengers are created equal, and is incorporating it into his thinking. He does a good job of explaining why he needs to segment customers.

Candidate: Let's assume that business travelers carry two bags on average: a laptop bag and another one, which is most likely also a carry-on bag. In reality, the average is probably somewhere between one and two as some business trips are day trips, but let's keep the math simple for now and assume two bags per passenger. Next, let's consider the leisure travelers' luggage. When I travel for leisure, I usually plan to stay away for at least 2 nights—if I am going away on vacation it is usually for a longer period of time requiring more luggage. Leisure travelers typically carry more luggage than business travelers, so let's assume a total of three bags per passenger. Finally, let's assume that 30 percent of passengers are business travelers. So the average number of bags per passenger is (30 percent are business travelers **x** 2 bags per passenger) + (70 percent are leisure travelers **x** 3 bags per passenger) = 0.6 + 2.1 = 2.7 bags per passenger. Let's round that down to 2.5 bags per passenger.

The candidate does a good job here showing that he is not afraid of using numbers, but is sure to use simple numbers so as not get tripped up trying to do the math in his head. It's also appropriate to justify each of the numbers you create so the interviewer understands how you arrived at them. It can be as simple as saying most business professionals travel with two bags: a laptop case and an overnight bag.

Candidate: So we now have an estimate for the amount of luggage each passenger is carrying. Next, we need to know how many passengers are traveling.

The candidate is summarizing where he is in the process and what the next step is. This is always a good idea if the process is lengthy or involved. Remember, outlining up front and maintaining a clear structure throughout the case are critical to moving to the next round and winning the job!

Candidate: The number of passengers traveling is equal to the number of passengers on a plane, multiplied by the number of planes taking off or landing at the airport each day. I have never been to San Francisco airport before, so I am not sure how big it is. Is it reasonable to assume that there are two runways?

On occasion, it is okay to reality check assumptions with your interviewer, although beware that she may throw the question right back at you.

Interviewer: Yes, I believe that the San Francisco airport does actually have two runways.

Candidate: Great. Well, let's assume that a plane takes off or lands every 5 minutes during the hours that the runway is operational. That is 60 divided by 5 = 12 planes per hour per runway, which is 24 planes per hour. Let's round that down to 20 per hour to take into account peak times vs slower times, delays, weather, etc. Let's also assume that the runways are open from 5 a.m. to 1 a.m.—20 hours a day. So the total number of planes we have arriving and departing is 20 hours **x** 20 planes per hour = 400 planes per day. So now that we know the number of planes, we still need one final piece of information: How many passengers are on each plane? Another tricky question because planes come in a number of sizes, including the big 747 plane and the smaller 737 plane. To avoid getting too complicated, I am going to assume that, on average, a plane holds about 200 people.

It is critical that the candidate come to a definitive answer, despite all the assumptions and calculations the question may require sifting through. The number should be in the right ballpark, but this is in no way an exact science, so you should not be concerned about getting exact figures.

Interviewer: Before we continue I would like to spend a moment talking about the assumption that you have made for total number of passengers on each plane. How comfortable are you with this assumption?

In this instance, the interviewer is challenging the candidate's assumption. This is not a cause for concern. Instead, use it is an opportunity to demonstrate how you respond to challenges and to further improve your calculation.

Candidate: Well, let me think about it for a moment . . .

When an interviewer questions something, take a moment and think about it. Do not simply jump in with a yes or no answer.

Candidate: A smaller shuttle-sized plane has about 25 rows of six seats, which equals 150 passengers. I also know that the big 747s hold well over 400 passengers, so without knowing more about the proportion of large planes to small planes I think that it is fair to assume that, on average, a plane can carry 200 people. However, not every plane is full. In fact, most of the time when I fly the plane isn't full. I would guess that, on average, planes fly 75 percent full, so that would mean that there are 75 percent x 200 = 150 passengers on each plane. That sounds like a more reasonable number.

The candidate does a nice job of grounding the initial assumption made with additional facts. He also recognizes and incorporates additional ideas, revising his assumptions accordingly. He demonstrates a willingness to revisit and refine assumptions.

Candidate: Now we can calculate the total number of bags. If you remember, we assumed there would be 400 planes a day and 150 passengers per plane, which gives us a total of 60,000 passengers traveling through San Francisco airport. We also assumed the average bags per passenger to be 2.5. So the total pieces of luggage is 60,000 x 2.5 = 150,000 pieces.

Try to make sure that the number you have ended up with sounds reasonable. Ground it against any facts that you have. If your number doesn't sound reasonable, be sure to say so—and then revisit your assumptions to try and determine why. If it doesn't sound reasonable to you, it probably doesn't sound reasonable to the interviewer either.

Interviewer: That sounds like a reasonable estimate. I don't know what the actual number is. Now, if I wanted to refine my calculation how might I do that?

Candidate: There are a number of different ways that you could refine this calculation, some of which we touched on briefly already. You could refine the way we are looking at passenger type. In this calculation, I looked at business passengers vs leisure passengers. You could also look at the length of trip they are making as a way to further segment these groups. Another option would be to look more closely at the type and size of planes and potentially their destinations (long-haul vs short-haul).

Mentioning just a few ways to refine your calculations is all it takes. Time is limited, and no one is expecting you to come up with every possible answer during a single interview.

Interviewer: Great job!

The candidate did a nice job answering the case. He clearly articulated his approach to the problem, kept the numbers simple, and grounded his assumptions when possible. He also made sure to share his thinking with the interviewer, ensuring that the interviewer did not have to guess what he was thinking at any point in time.

CASE 2

How many new golf balls are sold each year? Only consider golf balls sold to individuals (e.g., exclude golf balls sold at ranges).

Bad Answer

I don't play golf. That sport is for old, rich people with nothing better to do.

As in the prior market-sizing case, it is never a good idea to punt on a case interview question. In addition, never make pejorative statements: It is likely that the interviewer is an avid golfer if she is asking you this question.

Good Answer

Candidate: Well, I don't play a lot of golf myself, so you may need to help me with some of my assumptions, but I think that together we can figure out how to answer the question.

The candidate has done two things well in this response: 1) He has been up front about enlisting help from the interviewer in answering the question, and 2) He has demonstrated comfort with figuring out a problem in an area about which he doesn't know a lot.

Candidate: First of all, let's put some boundaries on the question. You asked how many new golf balls are sold each year. What sort of geography are we talking about? A city? The United States? The world?

Interviewer: Good question, I forgot to mention that. Let's just talk about golf balls in the United States.

Score one for the candidate.

Candidate: Okay. There are going to be two components to this exercise. First we have to figure out how many golfers there are, and then we have to determine how many golf balls the average golfer purchases over the course of the year.

Interviewer: Sounds like a decent proposal to me. Let's get going.

Clearly stating how you are going to approach the problem will allow the interviewer to prevent you from going down a wrong path. In this case, the candidate is structuring the case appropriately, and the interviewer has recognized that.

Candidate: So, how many golfers are there in the United States? The easy way to get to an answer would be to multiply the percentage of the population that plays golf by 300 million, or the rough number of people in the United States. However, I don't have a good sense of what the percentage is, so let's try to break down the problem a little further.

At this point the interviewer is probably wondering where exactly this is going, but is not going to interrupt until after the candidate makes his point.

Candidate: From what I can tell, you can play golf for most of your life—let's say from the time you're 10 to the time you're 70. Just to make the numbers easy, let's say that that segment is 80 percent of the population, or about 250 million people. If I were doing this for real, I'd be able to get this data from the census bureau.

The candidate has hit a home run here (with apologies for mixing baseball analogies with a golf case). He has begun to segment the population into a reasonable—or addressable—market. More importantly, he has made some simplifying assumptions and identified where he would find the data. The fact that people over 70 do play golf is less relevant here, and the interviewer will not hold that against the candidate.

Candidate: So the total number of people who *could* play golf is 250 million. The tricky part is determining how many of the 250 million actually do play. My guess is that it's fairly low, about 5 percent.

Interviewer: And why do you say that?

Candidate: Well, from the little I know about golf, there are a couple of things that keep it from being a widely popular sport. First of all, it is expensive: This will keep a segment of the population away from the game altogether. Second, it takes a long time to play: My friends who golf seem to be gone for most of the day when they play. So people who have other responsibilities—small children, for example—may not be able to dedicate a whole day to playing golf. Third, golf courses require large tracts of land: It's going to be difficult for people who live in large cities to play regularly. Lastly, golf is a pretty difficult and frustrating game from what I understand. I imagine that there are some people who can afford to play, don't have other commitments, and live close to golf courses who just choose not to play. These factors limit the number of potential players.

Interviewer: I agree with you on the first and last points: Golf is expensive and maddening, and this makes a large segment of the population stay away from the game altogether. However, the second two topics that you bring up would seem to address the frequency of playing, not the total number of players.

The interviewer is challenging the candidate on his assumptions. The key thing to do in this case is to understand the challenge and respond in a composed and articulate manner. The last thing you want to do is become flustered and panic.

Candidate: I see where you're going here. I was confusing the number of people who play with how often they play. So let's stick with the two factors that I did identify that limit the addressable market: the cost and the difficulty of the game. These are pretty significant, so can we stick with the 5 percent estimate?

Well done. The candidate recognized his error and has moved on.

Interviewer: Sure, let's go with that number.

Candidate: Okay. So 5 percent of 250 million is 12.5 million golfers. Now we need to determine how many golf balls these golfers buy per year. Again, let's segment the population to get a better understanding of what the differences are between these 12.5 million people. There's likely a spectrum of players here: some play all the time, others almost never. To simplify, let's say that there are three segments: the *frequent player*, the *sometimes player*, and the *rarely player*. Let's say that the frequent player is 15 percent of the golfing population, the sometimes player is 60 percent, and the rarely player is 25 percent. So, doing the math, there are roughly 2 million frequent players, 7.5 million sometimes players, and 3 million rarely players.

Great job of further segmenting the market. Also, don't think that you need to do all this math in your head; using a calculator or doing some quick calculations with a pen and paper is fine.

Candidate: Now we need to determine how often these segments play. The reason I need this information is because I'm going to calculate how many balls are needed per round. This will give me a more accurate calculation than just assuming an overall number of new balls per golfer per year.

It's important to keep the interviewer in the loop on your logic path, and the candidate explains his thinking well in this example.

Candidate: Let's say the frequent player plays three times a month, or 36 times a year. So 36 rounds per player x 2 million players is 72 million rounds of golf per year. For simplification, let's call that 70 million rounds. Let's assume that the sometimes player plays once a month, or 12 times a year. So 12 rounds per player x 7.5 million players is 90 million rounds. And let's say that the rarely player plays four times a year, or 12 million rounds (equal to 3 million players x four times per year). So that's 172 million rounds per year.

Hopefully the candidate is keeping all of these numbers written down, because there are a lot of numbers flying around at once.

Interviewer: Nice work. I see where you're going here and let me give you some helpful data. Let's assume that the frequent player needs three balls per round, the sometimes player needs six balls per round, and the rarely player needs ten balls per round.

Candidate: And I'm assuming the number goes up because the less you play, the more balls you lose.

Interviewer: Correct.

Candidate: All right. So the total number of balls that the frequent player segment uses is 7 million x 3 balls per round, or 21 million balls; for the sometimes player it's 9 million x 6 balls per round, or 54 million; and for the rarely player it's 12 million x 10 balls per round, or 120 million. So, 21 + 54 + 120 = 195 million balls.

Interviewer: So is that your answer?

Hint: the answer is going to be no.

Candidate: Well, you asked about new balls. This is the total number of balls that are used. When I was a kid I used to walk with my parents when they played golf and go in the bushes to find old golf balls. Then I'd sell them to my parents, so I imagine there's probably a big market for used balls as well.

Interviewer: Correct. If you were to give a rough estimate, what do you think the breakdown is between new and used balls? And what does this mean for the number of new balls that are purchased?

Candidate: This is going to be a wild guess, but let's say that the split is 20 percent old balls, 80 percent new balls. So this means that 80 percent of 195 million balls, or roughly 150 million balls, are new.

Interviewer: And how would you get a better sense of this number?

Candidate: One thing to do would be to interview a bunch of golfers. Another option would be to go to a pro shop that sells used balls and ask them what their split is between old and new balls.

Interviewer: Thanks. Does this case make you any more interested in golf?

See you at the second round!

CASE 3

It's a hot summer weekend day. How many movie tickets are purchased at the local theater?

This is a straightforward question with a couple of small twists. To quote Dr. Evil: "Pretty standard, really."

Bad Answer

Well, if there are four theaters and each theater holds about 200 people, then there are 800 people at each movie. If movies show five times a day, then there are 4,000 people purchasing movie tickets. That was easy—give me another one!

The candidate shows an ability to do some quick math, but makes too many quick assumptions for his answer to be acceptable.

Good Answer

Candidate: Okay. First, I want to put some boundaries on the question. You mentioned that it is a hot summer day: Are you looking for tickets only sold during the daytime? Or do you want the number of tickets for a 24-hour period?

Good start.

Interviewer: I'm looking for tickets sold over a 24-hour period.

Candidate: Got it. Let me give you a roadmap of how I'm going to solve this case. First, we need to evaluate how many screens this movie theater has. Then we need to determine how many seats there are in each theater. Then we need to figure out how utilized the theaters are—this will vary both by theater and by time. And finally we need to figure out how many showings there are on each of the screens. Once we have this information, we should be able to do all of the math to make an educated estimate of the number of tickets.

The interviewer is probably thinking, "When can we make an offer to this guy?" The candidate summarizes his logic very well and lays out the various information that he will need to crack the case. He also demonstrates an understanding of one of the subtleties of the case—that the capacity utilization of the theaters varies over the course of the day.

If you summarize like this, make sure you write everything down so, later, you don't forget your excellent logic!

Candidate: The first piece of data I need is the number of screens this theater has. Is this information that you can give me or do you want me to make an assumption?

Interviewer: Why don't you make a guess.

Candidate: You mentioned that it is a local movie theater. So I'm not going to assume that it's one of those 24-screen multiplexes. For round numbers, let's go with five screens.

Interviewer: Sounds good to me. From now on, you can refer to screens as theaters.

Two things to note here. First, the candidate clearly listened attentively to the initial question and picked up on the local theater reference. Second, he used that information to make an assumption that will help him keep the numbers easy. Multiplying by 5 is a lot easier than multiplying by 7 or 9 or 24!

Candidate: The next thing we need to figure out is how many seats there are in each theater—and there will probably be differences between them. There's likely going to be one or two large theaters where they're showing the new releases, and then there are likely some smaller theaters where the older movies are playing. Is this true at this theater?

The candidate continues to identify the key drivers of cracking the case.

Interviewer: It is. There is one large theater, two medium theaters, and two small theaters.

Candidate: Okay. So let's assess their relative sizes. The large theaters that I'm thinking of have about 50 rows with about 25 seats across. So, that makes 1,250 seats. Yikes—that number seems too high, so let's scale it back. Let's assume that there are 40 rows with 20 seats in each row. That adds up to 800 seats. Frankly, that still seems a little high, but let's stick with that number.

One way to score brownie points is to self check your answers, as the candidate does here. If they don't make sense, then say so. Doing these sanity checks will be important to your success in consulting. Also, don't worry if you can't do this math in your head. Just punch the numbers into your trusty calculator.

Candidate: The medium theaters might have 30 rows with 15 seats across, or 450 seats, and the small theaters might have 20 rows with 15 seats across, or 300 seats.

Interviewer: I agree with your logic. For simplicity, let's say that the large theater holds 500 people, the medium theaters hold 250 people, and the small theaters hold 100 people.

A gift from the interviewer! Remember that the number you ultimately come to on these market-sizing cases is less relevant than the logic you used to get there.

Candidate: Thanks—that makes things easier! Now we need to determine how many people are actually in the theaters for each showing. And, as I mentioned, this is going to differ by time of day and by type of movie. For example, the 8:30 p.m. showing in the large theater is going to be packed—particularly on a hot summer day when the latest Tom Cruise movie is out. However, the first showing of the day in the smaller theater is not going to be that full.

Interviewer: So how do we go about making some assumptions?

Candidate: Let's split up the viewing times into three buckets—morning, afternoon, and evening—and determine average capacity utilization by time and by theater.

Interviewer: If that's what you want to do, that's fine. But it may get a little complicated now that you have so many variables floating around: number of theaters, type of theater, time of day, capacity utilization. Can you simplify?

The interviewer is giving the candidate an out here and allowing him to make some simplifying assumptions. Take advantage of these should they happen! And note that, if the candidate hadn't structured the case so well up front, the interviewer would be less willing to help the candidate.

Candidate: Sure. Let's assume that there are only two buckets—peak and off-peak. Peak shows would be the ones that occur, say, after 4 p.m.

Interviewer: That's a reasonable assumption.

Candidate: Is there any data that you can give me on utilization for the peak and off-peak times?

Even in market-sizing questions, it's fine to ask for data. The interviewer can always say no.

Interviewer: I can give you one piece of data that will hopefully help you make more assumptions. The big theater has an average capacity utilization of 90 percent for peak times and 50 percent for off-peak times.

Candidate: Okay, so that means if its capacity is 500, then there are 450 tickets sold to the peak shows and 250 tickets sold to the off-peak shows.

Interviewer: Right. And how would you use the data I just gave you to make assumptions about the other types of theaters?

Candidate: Well, there are two ways to go here. One way to look at this would be to say that the utilization rates shouldn't change by theater because of the overall smaller capacity. The other way to look at it would be to say that the utilization rates will be lower because the movies are not as new.

Interviewer: What's your best guess?

Candidate: I think that the utilization rates will be slightly lower. And this data would be easy to get, if you're willing to sit at the movies all day and go from theater to theater. To make the numbers easy to calculate, let's assume that both the medium and small theaters have the same capacity utilization, and that it's 75 percent at peak and 50 percent at off-peak. So, for the medium theaters, it's roughly 190 people at peak and 125 people at off-peak. And, for the small theaters, it's 75 people at peak and 50 people at off-peak.

You'd better be writing these down, or you're going to drown in the numbers!

Candidate: The last thing we need to do is determine the number of showings. The number of showings is determined by the length of the movie, but let's say that—over time—the movie length is the same across all the theater types. Further, let's say that there are five showings a day: 10 a.m., 1 p.m., 4 p.m., 7 p.m., and 10 p.m. So there are three peak showings and two off-peak showings.

Interviewer: Okay. Then we should have all the data we need. What's your final answer?

The interviewer has been watching too much Regis *while in his hotel room in Des Moines.*

Candidate: I'll take this slow.

The candidate proceeds to write all of this out on paper, relying heavily on his calculator.

Candidate:

Large theater (peak) = 3 showings x 450 tickets per show = 1,350 tickets

Large theater (off-peak) = 2 showings x 250 tickets per show = 500 tickets

Total: 1,850 tickets

Medium theater (peak) = 3 showings x 190 tickets per show = 570 tickets

Medium theater (off-peak) = 2 showings x 125 tickets per show = 250 tickets

Total: 820 tickets x 2 theaters = 1,640 tickets

Small theater (peak) = 3 showings x 75 tickets per show = 225 tickets

Medium theater (off-peak) = 2 showings x 50 tickets = 100 tickets

Total: 325 tickets x 2 theaters = 650 tickets

1,850 + 1,640 + 650 = 4,140 tickets

Interviewer: That's fantastic work.

CASE 4

How many pounds of potatoes does McDonald's buy each week to support its U.S. operations?

This is a relatively straightforward question that could be used with either an undergraduate or advanced-degree candidate. Note, however, that there are a number of nuances that only a stronger candidate will recognize.

Bad Answers

- I don't cook and so I don't have any idea how McDonald's makes its french fries. I can't possibly answer that question. Can you give me a question that isn't about cooking?

The candidate does not typically get to choose which questions he answers. It is never smart to refuse to answer a question. It would be better to try and work through the question instead. Excuses like the one given by the candidate above are lame and suggest to the interviewer that the candidate lacks the ability to think outside of his comfort zone—rarely in consulting are you ever given a problem that you know intimately.

- The answer is zero. McDonald's doesn't use real potatoes to make its french fries. They are completely artificial.

If you are typically the class clown, this isn't the time to be a smart aleck. Employers want to hire professionals who take them and their interview process seriously. (And yes, McDonald's does indeed use real potatoes in every french fry.)

- McDonald's is disgusting. Did you see *Super Size Me* or that *Wall Street Journal* article about the person who left some McDonald's food outside on their patio in the sun for 2 weeks and it looked exactly the same as the day they bought it? Gross! I don't eat any fast food and I never have. In fact, I'd never set food in a McDonald's, so I can't possibly answer your question.

The candidate sounds like a snob refusing to lower himself to think about a McDonald's case. Also, pointing out the most negative aspect of companies your interviewer may have worked for isn't a sure way to success.

Good Answer

Candidate: Interesting question! Are you interested in all products that McDonald's makes with potatoes, i.e., hash browns, french fries, etc.?

Interviewer: Good question. Let's just focus on the french fries at the moment, since they will account for the bulk of potatoes purchased.

Candidate: Okay, I guess the way that I am going to approach this is to work out how many french fries you can make with one pound of potatoes. Then I will work out how many fries are produced by McDonald's each week. Then the total number of fries divided by the fries per pound of potatoes will tell me how many potatoes McDonald's needs to buy in any given week.

Structure! Structure! Structure! Remember to take a moment to think about how you want to structure your answer before you start. In this example, the candidate does a nice job of laying out his proposed approach in a concise and simple manner.

Candidate: One more clarifying question before we get started: Is it okay to assume that I am just calculating the volume based on french fries sold? McDonald's, for example, might be buying additional potatoes to increase their inventory levels.

When in doubt, ask! It is always a good idea to ask clarifying questions instead of simply making assumptions. If the interviewer does not want to answer your question she will communicate that to you and you can simply make an assumption (out loud) about your question. If you don't communicate the fact that you are making an assumption to your interviewer, she may just assume that you've missed a critical piece of the case.

Interviewer: Yes, that is correct. I am interested in knowing how many potatoes McDonald's need to support its french fry sales each week. Ignore any changes in inventory.

Candidate: Let's start by working out how many french fries you can make with a pound of potatoes. Potatoes come in all shapes and sizes. Let's assume that McDonald's uses those big potatoes and that there are five of them in a pound. They make quite skinny french fries, so I could probably make about 50 fries (seven slices by seven slices) from each potato. So, five potatoes per pound x 50 fries per potato gives me 250 fries per pound of potatoes bought.

The candidate tells you exactly what he is going to do before he does it, keeping the candidate and the interviewer aligned. He also isn't afraid to do some math, but sticks to simple numbers to avoid getting caught up by complicated arithmetic.

Candidate: Now, at this point we have assumed that all the potatoes in the batch that McDonald's purchased are fine. This probably isn't very realistic as I am sure that every so often they come across a dud potato and have to throw it away. I would guess that one in every 1,000 potatoes, or 1 in every 250 pounds of potatoes is bad. Given this is such a small percentage, let's ignore it for the moment.

The candidate identifies a nuance that might affect the calculation instead of just assuming it away. This demonstrates depth of thought to the interviewer.

Candidate: So, we now know how many french fries can be made with 1 pound of potatoes. The next step is to work out how many french fries McDonald's produces in a given week. I will get to this number by working out how many french fries a single store uses and multiply that by the number of stores. Now, I imagine that there is some variation in french fry sales over the year driven by special promotions and seasonal fluctuations. Is it okay to assume that this is just an average week with nothing special going on?

The candidate makes a point of frequently summarizing his progress with the calculations and the next steps. This is a good idea whenever you are focused on a long or multifaceted calculation. Not only does it ensure that the interviewer is still following along, but it also reminds you of the different steps so that you don't miss anything.

Interviewer: That sounds fine. Let's just assume that this is an average week.

Candidate: Let's focus first of all on the actual french fries. Now, I believe that McDonald's sells fries in four different size containers—small, medium, large, and extra large. Since the medium packet is sold as part of the standard value meal option, I would guess that that is the most popular size sold. Although, we do have an increasing problem with obesity in the United States so maybe the most popular size is a bit larger. For simplicity's sake, let's assume the average size sold is the medium box. Let's also assume that a medium box holds about 50 french fries. I have never counted the number of french fries in a box of fries, but I figure a potato would probably fill a box, particularly after the skin is peeled off. Now, we know how many french fries are in a box of fries, so, next we need to work out how many boxes are sold. To do this, we need to think for a moment about the stores selling the fries.

It is okay to let the interviewer know that you are making an educated guess. Always try and explain the basis for your guess so the interviewer knows that it is an educated one, and not pulled out of thin air. Ground all numbers you use in any way possible!

Candidate: McDonald's stores can probably be segmented in a number of different ways based on size, location, etc. In this case, let's try segmenting stores into high-volume stores and low-volume stores. This is probably a function of where they are located—a densely populated area is likely to generate more sales than a low-density area, despite the higher amount of competition they likely face. Are you comfortable with me using two segments of stores?

Interviewer: Yep.

Rarely will an interviewer have a problem with your assumptions unless they are far off base or are steering the conversation in a direction the interviewer doesn't wish to go.

Candidate: Let's start with the high-volume stores, which I would think would be open 24-hours a day. The fry flow is going to vary throughout the day, with peak periods around meal times. During busy times like lunch they are probably selling multiple boxes a minute—say ten boxes per minute, or 600 boxes per hour. Sounds quite high, but you do see long lines there at lunchtime and the service is usually very quick. Busy times account for probably 3 to 4 hours of the day. Let's be generous and say 4 hours a day. During slow times they probably sell one box every 2 minutes or 30 boxes per hour. I would say this covers the other 20 hours of the day. So what does that give us for a day of sales? (30 boxes per hour x 20 hours) + (4 hours of busy time x 600 boxes per hour) = 600 boxes + 2,400 boxes = 3,000 boxes per day. This sounds fairly reasonable, as it would imply that 3,000 people visit a high-volume store, or about 125 people per hour, or a little over two people per minute—assuming of course that each person only buys one order of french fries!

Next, low volume stores. These stores are probably only open between 5 a.m. and, say, 11 p.m. (18 hours a day). In their peak hours, they probably do half the sales of the high-volume stores, so that is about 300 boxes per hour. During the slow times, they are probably quite a bit slower and sell maybe 10 boxes per hour. So a day of sales in a low-volume store equals (10 boxes per hour x 14 hours) + (200 boxes x 4 hours of peak time) = 140 + 800 = 940 boxes per day—let's round up to 1,000 boxes a day for simplicity's sake.

Okay, so the next question before we move on: What are our average daily sales of french fries? To get to that we need to know what proportion are high-volume stores vs low-volume stores. Well, this is not something that I have a really good feel for so I am going to use the 80/20 percent rule as a starting point, and assume that 20 percent are high-volume stores and the other 80 percent are low-volume stores. That would mean an average store volume would be 80 percent x 1,000 boxes + 20 percent x 3,000 boxes = 800 + 600 = 1,400. So, let's say an average store sells 1,400 boxes of fries a day. Before we go on let's convert that to pounds of potatoes. 1,400 boxes of fries x 50 fries per box = 70,000 french fries a day. 70,000 french fries divided by 250 fries per pound of potatoes = 280 pounds of potatoes per store per day. McDonald's stores are open 7 days a week, so that is 280 pounds per day x 7 days = 1,960 pounds per week.

This candidate is rolling in calculations!

Candidate: So, now we know the pounds of potatoes sold per store per day, but we still need to know how many stores McDonald's has in the United States. I am going to guess there are somewhere between 10,000 and 15,000 McDonald's restaurants across the states. Let's go with 10,000 for now. So 10,000 stores x 1,960 pounds of potatoes = 19,600,000 pounds of potatoes per week.

When you are asked to estimate something it is important that you actually end up with an estimate number, in this case the number of pounds of potatoes. Always ask yourself whether or not your answer sounds reasonable, and if not, revisit your assumptions to try and come to a more realistic conclusion.

Interviewer: That sounds like a reasonable number to me. Can you think of any factors that might affect it?

Candidate: Well, we talked about some of the things that might affect it earlier. We discussed how some of the potatoes might not be useable, meaning that you have to buy extra potatoes to meet your french fry needs. In addition, some of the french fries produced may not be saleable because they have sat on the counter too long, or they have been returned by customers. I imagine that McDonald's is pretty good at minimizing waste and so, all in all, this probably adds maybe 1 percent or so to the total.

If the interviewer asks you to try and identify some additional factors, don't panic. This is not an indication that you have not answered the question in a well thought out structured manner. The interviewer is simply taking the question to the next level and finding out if you have thought at all about how you might refine your calculations. While it is important to try and come up with at least one suggestion here, you do not need to go overboard.

Interviewer: Great job. Now we are going to switch gears and talk about something a little bit different.

The candidate does a great job with this case. He applies a structure early on in the question and sticks to it. He also makes a point of frequently summarizing his progress with the case and his next steps, thus keeping himself aligned with the interviewer. The candidate also does a good job of highlighting the assumptions he is making and grounding them out loud whenever possible, demonstrating that he is comfortable doing this even when the material is not familiar to him.

Business Operations Case Questions

CASE 5

The president of a large pencil and pen company has hired your consulting company to assess why profits have fallen from respectable levels 4 years ago to a net loss this year. You have been assigned the role of main business analyst on the engagement. You have enough information to know that the client has some kind of operations issue at play that has increased expenses and eroded profitability—but no one knows what the issue is. How would you go about analyzing the situation and assessing the source(s) of this company's operations problem?

This is a commonly asked case question about the potential reasons for and responses to a drop in profits. You'll encounter questions like this referring to various industries, but the approach to solving them is similar. When you are provided enough information in the setup to know that it's an operations question—and not a market strategy or any other category of question—you'll want to structure your approach in a way that is optimized to get to the bottom of the operations issues at hand.

Bad Answer

Candidate: I'd basically just find out what the problem is by talking to all of the company's employees and doing a bunch of observations of its manufacturing processes. I studied operations enough in school that I am really good at identifying costly manufacturing inefficiencies. Then, my consulting team and I would just tell them how to fix that part of their manufacturing line so that it doesn't cost as much to operate.

Wow, that's really specific. Thanks for the overview of how operations analysis and consulting works. . . . Avoid extremely general answers. You need to focus on THIS business problem, not all business problems—and suggesting that the problem will be pretty trivial to solve once you see their manufacturing process is naïve. It also belittles the supposed intelligence of the managers of the theoretical client—which no consulting firm wants to see in a junior employee, as it would signal potential problems in client-relationship management down the road if they were to hire you.

Interviewer: Yes, that is basically what we might do as a consulting team if we were to get the engagement. But what would you focus on in this case to get more specific about the source of the operations problem that this client is having—how would you go about it in more exact terms?

The interviewer was tactful in delivering the message: "Get on with it—let me see how you think."

Candidate: Well, it seems to me that pencils are pretty easy to make, since all they require is wood and pencil lead. I'm pretty sure that if it's suddenly costing the company more to make pencils, and its not making as much money this year, then the issue is that the wood and pencil lead must be costing more to acquire. I'd recommend that the company figure out how to get cheaper wood and pencil lead from some other suppliers—then costs would come down and it'd start making money again.

This candidate will be writing more cover letters with pens rather than pencils soon enough if she continues down this track. Guessing at the heart of the problem without gathering any background information is always a bad idea—it's the equivalent of shooting at a target in a dark room. You might hit the target, but in all likelihood you won't. Whatever the outcome of the guessing game, the answer isn't really the point in operations or other case interview questions like this one—the process by which the candidate thinks her way through the problem at hand is. More information is needed here before any prospective answer can be theorized and suggested, and the candidate should have tempered the urge to skip ahead to a recommendation before investigating the situation.

Good Answer

Candidate: If profits are down, and the core of the problem is known to lie somewhere in the operations and manufacturing processes of the company, then I can assume that revenue is flat or up, and that the heart of the problem is instead on the cost side of this company's equation. I'd want to validate this, to make sure there aren't any other market forces impacting the situation and driving sales down to a point where economies of scale are less effective than they had been at a higher pencil output rate in the past. Can you confirm that this is the case, and that I should be focusing my investigation of this problem on the costs of production for this client? I'd like to know if revenue and pricing have been roughly constant over the time period in question.

The candidate has successfully recognized this as a profit question, and has introduced the profit equation. Further, the candidate has taken a safe and conservative step by validating that this is a case to focus on the costs rather than revenue side of the profitability equation. It's smart and prudent when first entering a case to demonstrate that you understand what makes companies profitable—and what the potential sources of problems can be.

Interviewer: Good job making sure you're clear on what the client knows already, and confirming that. Yes, you've got it right: Revenue has been flat over the last 5 years and during that time period the price of its pencils has been constant as well, so that's not the source of the problem. Margins were looking pretty good until recently, but costs have been up in the last year.

So the issue to further investigate is costs of production. The candidate should proceed along those lines and dig deeper.

Candidate: Okay, so if the problem is fundamentally on the cost side, then I'd like to learn a little more about the components of its cost equation for pencil production. Can you tell me if the cost of the raw goods the company acquires has increased lately?

The candidate has wisely decided to start by understanding the current dynamics of the industry and digging into one of the most obvious potential problems: cost increases due to exogenous or external market forces. If there are macro issues affecting the client's business—cost increases for raw goods, for example—these could translate directly to increased costs and shrinking profit margins for the finished goods, if all other costs in the production equation are staying constant.

Interviewer: Actually, we've looked into the market, and the cost of acquiring the raw materials required to make pencils has stayed constant.

Now the candidate should dig into other potential sources of cost of production, since she knows it's not the cost of the product inputs.

Candidate: All right. Now I'd want to know more about the other costs of production. I assume that the manufacturing process involves both people and machinery. Has anything changed in the last year that would impact these costs—such as the failure of any of the machines?

The candidate is starting to test a theory—that one of the core operations costs, such as labor or manufacturing cost, has increased in the past year.

Interviewer: Well, I can tell you that none of the machines have failed, and the manufacturing process is the same as it ever was—just as efficient in terms of output, and just as costly in terms of electricity and other maintenance costs to keep the machines running.

The candidate continues to make good progress through her framework of examining the elements or components of manufacturing costs. Since the interviewer appears to have intentionally NOT touched on labor costs, it might merit digging deeper to make sure there isn't something happening worth further investigation.

Candidate: Right. So how about the workforce and labor costs? That can often be a big source of the operations cost for a traditional manufacturer. Any changes in the last year there?

Interviewer: Well, now that you ask, I can tell you that the president of the company recently informed us that the workforce at one of its key pencil production plants was unionized early last year.

This is a key piece of data that wasn't shared earlier in the case discussion. This is typical of a case—while the key piece of information is important to understanding the problem and addressing it, it often is intentionally obscured or not shared early on so that the candidate MUST dig enough to uncover it and benefit from considering how it would impact the problem.

Candidate: Okay, that's interesting. Can you tell me, did the unionization result in any changes to labor contracts or salaries for that portion of the company's workforce?

Good follow-up.

Interviewer: Yes, in fact, it did. After that portion of the labor force unionized, their union representatives were successful in negotiating a 40 percent increase in salaries and paid benefits from the company.

Now the candidate seems to be at the heart of the matter—an increase in labor costs that's directly impacting the profitability of the company's manufacturing function.

Candidate: Very interesting. What portion of the total production costs is represented by the labor costs, and what were the approximate profit margins before this unionization occurred?

Now the candidate is getting the last piece of information she needs to really analyze and assess the impact of this change in the company's operations and cost equations to profitability. Sometimes hard numbers are needed to really ensure that the right answer is being achieved.

Interviewer: Now that you ask, labor costs were about 55 percent of the total cost of production, and profit margins for its pencils averaged about 20 percent overall.

At this point, the candidate has received the quantitative and qualitative information necessary to properly issue an assessment of the source of the profitability problem and tie it to the operations of the company.

Candidate: Now that I know that, and I know the increase in labor costs, a back-of-the-envelope calculation tells me that this increase in labor prices has eliminated any profits and raised the cost of production of a pencil to a level higher than the price of that pencil. In short, it appears that this company has a labor-cost-increase problem that is responsible for its higher costs of production and the loss of profitability in its pencil division.

Good—the source of the problem has been reached and communicated. Now, in a longer case interview, the interviewer might ask the candidate her suggestions about what to actually do about it. After all, consultants are hired not only to identify the problem, but also to suggest tactics for how to address and, hopefully, resolve it for the future.

Interviewer: Good analysis—I think you've gotten to the bottom of the operating cost issue that this company is facing. Now, what are some ideas you'd suggest that our consulting team should examine in order to provide direction and possible solutions to this company?

At this point, the candidate does not need to have all the answers—instead, a few good ideas that sound logical and reasonable to investigate further are adequate. Most case interviewers don't expect their candidates to have the answers—just some creative ideas for which direction to head.

Candidate: Well, I'm not an expert in unions and labor negotiations, but here are a few ideas that come to mind given the nature of the problem we've identified here: First, I'd like to assess whether there is any leeway to reengage the union about the outcome of their recent contract negotiation, and see if there is any room to move the salaries and benefits back down closer to historical levels. Perhaps there is—especially if the contract is yearly and not longer in term. But, if there isn't, then there is a more challenging task: drastically reducing other operating costs involved in pencil production to compensate for the increase in the labor-cost portion of its profitability equation—to try to drive average unit production costs back down below the average unit price and restore some profitability. Along these lines, I'd want to investigate whether the manufacturing machines and processes could be improved or replaced to yield more efficient production. This might result in more output at lower overall manufacturing costs, which could help offset the higher labor costs going forward.

Finally, once all of the sources of cost had been investigated, if there were not clear opportunities to reduce any of the costs of production, then the company might need to investigate opportunities to raise pencil prices enough to restore an opportunity for profits on a per-unit basis, without eroding the demand for its pencils in the marketplace. If the producer were a monopoly or had sufficient market power, then this route might be easier because suppliers with that kind of market power don't face as much reduction in demand for their products when prices go up, as do those in highly competitive markets where there are alternative products of comparable quality available at lower prices. This would be where I'd start to look further into opportunities for the company—but, of course, I would need to spend the time and careful attention looking at each in turn before I suggested any one as a solution to the client.

Good. The candidate has demonstrated some solid thinking about potential ideas to investigate for the client, but has shown the patience and need for further investigation that is the hallmark of a good analyst and a top-quality consultant. While this answer may be more robust than what a typical candidate can come up with on the fly, it's provided to illustrate some of the possible ideas that a strong candidate would keep in the back of her mind, to surface once the source of the problem has been identified in an operations case like this one involving manufacturing.

CASE 6

The managing partner of one of the larger regional offices of a management consulting company is concerned because he has noticed an industry-wide reduction in consulting spending during the previous year. He is thinking about the impact this might have on how he runs his management consulting practice within his own office, and he has asked for your help in evaluating the problem. What would you like to know, and how would you advise this managing partner to react to his situation?

Changes in the marketplace for a good or service, and the likely impact of these changes on a particular company and its operational processes, are frequent sources of business operations case questions. The fact that this case covers the changes and likely responses within a management consulting company means that a truly successful interview candidate will not only show generalized knowledge of the operations of a professional services company, but also demonstrate some knowledge of how a management consulting company specifically is organized and managed.

Bad Answers

- I'd like to know where he is getting his information about management consulting services spending. I'm surprised that would be true—from everything that I have heard, business spending on management consulting services has been steadily growing. The first thing I would do is make sure that he has done enough research to really believe that spending on consulting is going to slow down.

Unless there is a very good reason, steer clear of starting out a case by doubting or questioning the information presented in the case itself. In general, you should trust whatever you are told by the interviewer to set up the case—these are not police investigations or murder mysteries, they are almost always very straightforward and structured in a way to simply get the candidate engaged in a discussion about general business principles. Focus on moving things forward throughout the case, rather than questioning the foundation of the case itself right off the bat.

- I think he better be pretty conservative and start planning to lay people off—getting rid of excess people is the first step towards making sure that you don't lose a ton of money when your market cools off.

This candidate moved to a recommendation MUCH too quickly—she hasn't investigated the issues at all. Until it is clear what the operational dynamics and concerns are for the managing director in this case, the candidate should avoid jumping to overconfident—and potentially callous or impractical—solutions.

Good Answer

Candidate: This is an interesting case since it involves a services company, rather than a manufacturing company, which means that the head of that office is going to be managing a different set of operations costs and processes. I'll assume that things aren't going to get better anytime soon and that the managing director's challenge is going to be cost containment in a changing environment of demand for his office's services. I think his concern is mainly going to be keeping fixed and variable costs of running his office at the appropriate level to ensure that his office can remain profitable if his revenues start to fall off.

This is a strong start. The candidate has inferred key information from the setup of the case—namely that the overall industry demand is contracting and that this is likely to negatively impact revenues. The candidate has further communicated that she understands the profit equation—and that costs, rather than revenues, are the relevant variable for the managing director's focus.

Interviewer: That's a safe assumption. When the overall industry is experiencing a downturn, management of the office's costs is the main operational concern, even though there are also strategic concerns about how to add new customers and create new demand for its services in the medium to long term. But for now, let's focus on the short term and what the managing director really needs to do.

So, the interviewer is validating that cost management is at the heart of the matter here. Move forward with considering and analyzing the operational costs that a company like this one would be working hardest to manage—i.e., which operational costs are the most significant or are the highest priority to manage in this particular case?

Candidate: In a general sense, I would want to think about how to manage the largest categories of fixed and variable costs that make up his office's operational expenses. Given what I know about consulting companies like this one, the main fixed costs tend to be things related to keeping the company running, such as accounting and IT departments, and the cost of administrative needs, like the HR and travel departments that keep its people organized and well supported. I would guess that these are harder to manage down to lower costs on a short-term basis, since these functions take a long time to invest in and, thereby, take a long time to reduce costs.

The candidate is continuing to show good knowledge of both the theory of operating costs and their practical application to a services business. Of course, a focus on fixed costs for a manufacturing company would include many of these as well as key additional fixed costs like plants, machinery, and other fixed assets related to the production of the goods.

Interviewer: Yes, that's probably a fair guess at some of the key fixed costs that this managing director faces. What are some of the other costs he should think about?

Candidate: He would also need to think about the variable costs he manages. For a professional services company like his, I think the main variable costs would be the salaries of the consulting staff that his office employs to actually do the consulting work supplied to his office's clients.

The candidate has correctly identified employee salaries as one of the main levers that the managing director has to manage variable operating costs. However, the candidate should identify one or two other variable costs just to be comprehensive and also to consider more than one possibility for impacting the cost side of the profitability equation.

Interviewer: Yes, employee salaries are a big component of the variable costs that the managing director needs to consider. Are there any others?

Candidate: Some of the other variable costs that a professional services company like this one might incur would include travel and expenses related to the consultants' client-service work, contractors and other part-time workers' compensation, maybe office supplies and other non-fixed assets used to run the business, and all the selling and R&D expenses related to finding new clients and developing new service offerings for that particular office of the company.

Interviewer: Good job—that's a pretty solid list of the fixed and variable costs that this managing director would want to be considering in thinking about how to address the operations of this office. So, what would you suggest he do in terms of focus areas and ideas for how to contain costs if his revenues are declining?

The interviewer wants to move the candidate to the point in the discussion where the candidate must leave the realm of the theoretical—the world of standard business theory—and enter the practical world specific to this situation. Necessarily, this means that the discussion is going to turn more subjective, and rely more on what the candidate thinks rather than knows. At this point, the interviewer wants to go deeper and really see what the candidate's practical business experience and instincts lead her to recommend.

Candidate: Well, let's consider each of the cost categories in turn. With regard to fixed costs, most of the costs I mentioned are relatively more difficult to reduce or impact on a short-term basis. It's the very fact that they are hard to change that makes us think of them as being fixed costs. If the managing director needed to make drastic changes, perhaps he could consider reducing the real estate budget by using less real estate space for existing staff. While this may not be popular, it might be possible to reduce the monthly real estate lease fees—or gain some subleasing rents if the company owns its headquarters' buildings and can free enough space to take on new tenants and make do with less space. This would be difficult to pull off politically because it might cause some morale issues among employees, especially permanent staff—and implementation of these sorts of changes might be slow, given the time it would take to rearrange the offices, find new tenants for the leases, etc.

If revenues were sharply declining, however, I could see the managing director trying to tighten the budget down for building and administrative costs—and explain why it was necessary for cost containment honestly to the staff. I know that the things that get cut first in annual budgets during economy downturns are "nonessential" spending and projects that aren't necessarily core to the selling and servicing of clients—like new technology expenditures, company perquisites, and incentive trips for top salespeople. The managing director might be able to reduce nonvital expenditures for the next several quarters in an effort to help profitability since revenues are falling. He would need to explain to the staff that he expects these cuts to be temporary, rather than permanent, while he and his team figure out a plan to increase revenues in the longer term. This might help cut some of the costs of the business.

Sometimes the candidate needs to go with her instincts and make a judgment call about where to focus her thinking and recommendations. This is fine to do—the interview time is limited, after all.

Interviewer: I can see why you might suggest some of these ideas about reducing the fixed costs for this managing director's office—those basically make sense—but, as you yourself admitted, these might take a long time to implement and benefits from in terms of cost reductions. Any other ideas that this managing director could evaluate and perhaps put into practice more quickly?

Occasionally in a case interview, the interviewer will help lead the candidate along without necessarily correcting or chastising her. In this case, the interviewer is focusing the candidate next on the variable costs since he wants to see how the candidate will think about this part of the problem.

Candidate: Yes, the other main source of expenses that I mentioned earlier was the salaries and other expenses for the full-time management consulting employees in this office. This is a much more tricky issue, since letting employees go during tough times does save money but also carries some expenses due to severance payments—not to mention that it's politically difficult and might even have negative PR consequences for that office and the company in general if it becomes too severe. However, if the managing director believes that the downturn in revenue and demand for his company's and his office's services is going to be prolonged, then taking this action makes sense so that the company doesn't bear the costs of underutilized consulting staff by paying them their high salaries while they are not generating revenues for the company and the office. Suggesting that the managing director consider laying off employees to reduce costs, while difficult to suggest under any condition, also assumes that the company's employees aren't unionized or employed under long-term contracts which prevent changes to the size of their labor force in the short term.

While firing employees does save money, it also brings with it new expenses that must be considered in evaluating the total impact of the changes on overall expenses. It's also no fun for anyone involved, and carries nonexpense considerations like PR and morale implications inside and outside the company. A savvy—and empathetic—businessperson always understands that the primary objective of company managers is to employ and keep the very best people. This awareness should never be lost, and should occasionally be acknowledged openly in any discussion about labor force reductions and employees being considered as a "cost of doing business."

Interviewer: Letting employees go could save the company significant money, assuming that their overall business is contracting. The managing director has actually been considering this step, as he does believe that the economy and the demand for his company's special type of management consulting could be in for a longer-term downturn. If the managing director accepted this recommendation, what else would you advise him to consider before he starts directing his managers to reduce their headcounts?

Candidate: First, I would want to assist him in building a solid analysis and business case for the need to reduce his consulting staff so that we're confident in the right amount of people to let go—no more and no few. It seems to me that such a drastic and emotional step for the company always needs to be done in a clear and well-thought-out, well-communicated, and well-supported manner, where the reductions in headcount make sense in size and timing, even if they are hard to hear.

Interviewer: Good. Okay, what else would you consider?

Candidate: Second, I would counsel him to communicate the headcount reduction plan to the management team of the parent company and to seek its input and advice before locking on the plan and starting to carry it out. Getting buy-in and support for his office-management plans seems very important when part of a larger company with other offices and employee bases.

Interviewer: That makes sense—company managers never like to be taken by surprise or find out that one of their managing directors is carrying out any major decisions without consulting them and getting their input first. What else would you want to consider?

Candidate: Third, since there are other nonfinancial, but nevertheless important, aspects of an employee base headcount reduction that I mentioned, I think it would be important that this managing director ensure that the parent company has a PR plan in place to address any questions which may arise from Wall Street and analysts, if the company is public, when the staff reductions become public knowledge. Finally, I would advise him to be open about the task at hand to all the stakeholders internally—and especially to make sure that HR was well equipped and knowledgeable so that they could handle the employees who were going to be let go with clear offers and direction. Since HR tends to be the first and last point of contact for employees, and an especially hard burden falls on their shoulders to handle the details of hirings and firings, I would want the managing director to feel confident that he had a strong HR team in place to help carry out the headcount reduction plan with empathy and the best exit plan that the company could afford for these employees.

Good job—Bonus points for showing a savvy understanding of the challenges of reducing employee expenses through layoffs. The more a candidate demonstrates knowledge of some of the more nuanced or challenging aspects of running a medium- to large-sized company—or even a subdivision or office of a large company—the more committed she appears to be to a long-term career and a personal investment in that industry. This can be valuable to demonstrate in a case interview in and of itself, so long as it's not poured on too thickly. Simply saying, "I really really want to be a management consultant," or "an investment banker," or "a consumer products marketer" is one thing . . . but to show you've invested your personal time in learning some of the intricacies of how a particular industry or role operates tells a much more effective story about your interest in and preparation for that kind of a job. You may not have the direct chance to show it off as blatantly as the example provided here, but any investment in learning the specific requirements and expectations of a role in a particular industry, as well as the basic hallmarks of effective management of the successful businesses in that industry, will shine through over the course of an interview and reflect well upon the candidate who invests this extra time.

Interviewer: Your suggestions make sense and would be a good basis for conversation with this managing director about the cost-reducing options ahead of him as he faces the challenge of managing the operations and costs of his office in the situation I described. Thanks for sharing your ideas with me.

CASE 7

The CEO of Bon Jeans, a famous jeans producer, has come to you for help with his retail division. His company sold jeans primarily through department stores until 2 years ago. Once that channel became saturated, the company decided to launch retail stores to capture additional sales. The stores got off to a flying start, but have recently been declining in profitability—to the point that the company's retail division has become unprofitable. What's making the stores unprofitable?

Bad Answers

- Well, obviously no one is buying his product because it sucks. He needs to fire his designer and find someone new who can design jeans that sell.

The candidate provides a shallow answer with little thought. There's rarely an easy answer to these questions—and if there is, you can never jump to the answer, even if you know it off-hand. The interviewer is interested in your thought process, not whether or not you get to the answer (although coming up with the answer is always an extra bonus). So, don't just blurt out an answer, particularly an obnoxious one like this.

- Jeans are really trendy: Sometimes they are cool and people buy them, and sometimes they're not. They should just hang in there.

The candidate's answer demonstrates a lack of maturity and thought. Consultants will never advise companies to "just hang in there." Yes, jeans and clothing are trendy, but there is a lot more to the industry (and all other industries) than this simplistic answer would suggest.

Good Answer

Candidate: This sounds like an interesting question. Let me just take a moment to think about how I might approach answering it.

For complicated questions like this, it's a very good idea to take a moment and pause. Give yourself a chance to put together a structured, coherent response. Think through the different frameworks that you could potentially use and identify the most appropriate one.

Candidate: Before we actually delve into the question of performance in the retail division, can I ask if this issue is just a retail division problem or is it affecting other parts of the business as well?

The candidate starts off by clarifying the scope of the question being addressed.

Interviewer: That is a good question. You can assume that performance in the department store division has remained strong over the time period in question. It has experienced steady sales growth and costs have remained relatively flat.

Every shred of information the interviewer provides is a clue to help the candidate resolve the case. Think carefully about the questions that you ask the interviewer. It is likely that he will only be willing to answer a certain number of questions, so use them wisely.

Candidate: Well, that would lead me to believe that the company's issue is not a market driven problem. It's also probably not a problem with the product either, as customers are buying the jeans through other channels. Okay, let's start to examine why profitability has declined. Profitability is a function of revenues and costs. If profitability has declined, then revenues have fallen, costs have risen, or some combination of the two has occurred. Has revenue declined in the retail store division?

The candidate clearly lays out her structured approach to the problem before digging in and asking questions. The interviewer should be well aware of the thought process you are using and where you are in that process at all times.

Interviewer: Total revenue in the division has remained flat.

Candidate: Okay, the fact that total revenue has remained flat could still be hiding something. To be sure that this is not a revenue problem, I think we need to delve a little deeper. You can break out total revenue in a lot of different ways. If we let total revenue equal revenue per store x total number of stores, then we can check to see what has happened to revenue per store. Has revenue per store also remained flat?

The candidate is smart enough to realize that there is more to revenue than the top-level number would reveal. She decides to delve a little deeper before moving on to another potential driver of the issue. In this case, she makes use of a simple structure to deconstruct revenue into its drivers—the number of stores and revenue per store—to see if there is a deeper problem lingering.

Interviewer: No, the revenue per store has declined.

Candidate: If the revenue per store has declined then that tells us the number of stores we operate must have increased to keep total revenue flat. Increasing the number of stores will have resulted in an increase in the cost base and that would explain the declining profitability. The big question is why has the revenue per store fallen? Is it that the new stores aren't performing as well as the old stores, or is it something else?

Let's start with the question of new stores vs old stores before we delve further into the store-performance questions. Is there any difference in the performance of the existing stores vs the new additional stores?

Again, the candidate continues to dive deeper into the problem, identifying the key drivers of each aspect of the issue she is exploring and then asking questions concerning that driver.

Interviewer: Basically, what seems to happen is whenever a new store is launched, it does well for the first month or two, and then it goes into decline and total sales in the store fall. All stores have exhibited the same pattern.

Candidate: Well, let's think about some of the different things that it could be: price, place, promotion, or product. Let's start with price: price per pair of jeans x number of jeans sold = revenue per store. Has the average price per pair of jeans changed?

This is a good use of one of the basic structures—the 4Ps—that you can use in an interview of this type. Using this approach will ensure that you cover all the basics, without missing out on something big. However, while a framework such as this may help you, do not feel like you must jam one in to each case interview you have—use only when appropriate.

Interviewer: No, the average price has remained flat.

Candidate: If the average price per pair of jeans has remained flat, then the stores must be selling fewer jeans. Why? Let's think about place next. Perhaps the stores are located in low footfall areas that can't generate enough sales to maintain the stores.

Interviewer: Actually, all of the stores are in fantastic locations. The company spent a lot of time identifying the right malls in which to locate. It picked high footfall, top revenue-generating malls for its stores. Here is some data about its performance in some of the different malls. Perhaps this will help you out.

Location	Average Sales per Sq. Ft. ($)	Bon Jeans Sales per Sq. Ft. ($)
The Galleria, Dallas TX	650	200
South Coast Plaza, CA	800	175
Oakbrook Shopping Centre, IL	625	300
The Mall at Millennia, FL	700	225

Don't get flustered with tables and charts of data. Try to discern the key message that is coming out of the information, without getting bogged down in the details.

Candidate: Thanks. Now let's see what the data is telling us. Basically, in every mall on the list, Bon Jeans is performing significantly worse than the other stores in the mall. So, for some reason, the client is not generating the same volume of sales as other stores in the mall. We have talked about price and place, so let's tackle promotion next. My guess here is that advertising activities would drive brand awareness and drive customers to all outlets selling Bon jeans. The fact that the department store division is experiencing strong sales suggests that the marketing is effective. The only caveat on that would be if marketing was specific to divisions and not done to drive overall brand awareness.

The candidate identifies and articulates the key message from the data table. She then incorporates the new data into her thinking and moves forward. It is always a good idea to talk through the data provided out loud. This demonstrates to the interviewer that you are able to understand, interpret, and use data effectively.

Interviewer: This is very true; the client focuses most of its marketing spending on building brand awareness. It does spend a small amount on store or department store–specific promotions, but this is not large enough to cause the decline that we have seen.

The interviewer is happy to discuss the case with the candidate. If he wanted the candidate to move forward more quickly with the case, he would make this known.

Candidate: This is a challenging problem. Let's recap what we know so far and see if that helps to shed light on the answer. We know that sales in retail stores have been declining. Other divisions of the company are experiencing growth, suggesting that it is not an issue with the product, changing consumer tastes, our promotional techniques, etc. We also know that the retail stores are located in high footfall, strong-performing malls—so why isn't the company able to sell more jeans? Let me ask you another question: I know that the stores are in high-footfall areas, but are customers actually going into the stores when they are in the mall?

The candidate perseveres. If at first you don't identify the answer, keep working at it. Stick to the framework that you have laid out and use a process of elimination. Eventually, you will get there!

Interviewer: Yes, the client is getting the number of customer store visits we would expect given its locations.

Candidate: So, the customer is coming into the store and leaving empty-handed. Let me back up a second and ask another question: If the customers in department stores are buying the jeans, but the ones in the retail stores aren't, maybe they are a different set of customers? Are different customer segments shopping in the two different channels—department stores and retail stores, that is?

While using a process of elimination, the candidate realizes that she may have missed something and backs up to incorporate it. It is always better to incorporate something than to just ignore it and potentially miss the point of the case altogether.

Interviewer: No. In general, the same type of consumer shops in retail and department stores. Both channels have roughly the same customer demographics.

Candidate: Well then, if the consumer wants to buy the product and is visiting the retail stores, then the stores must just not have the product to sell the customers. The retail stores must be running out of stock or experiencing inventory problems of some kind.

Interviewer: You have hit the nail on the head. Not experienced in running its own distribution channels, the Bon Jeans retail division has been plagued with inventory issues since its launch. The company has been unable to effectively manage the store inventory requirements—meaning that a lot of customers are walking away empty-handed when the store does not have their size available.

The candidate successfully navigates the case and identifies the reason for the decline in store profitability. She makes good use of frameworks (profit = revenue – cost) and the 4Ps (price, product, promotion, and place) to guide her answer.

Warning: Do not feel like you must bombard the interviewer with all the frameworks you have learned in your strategy class—use only what is appropriate and relevant. Just because you didn't use Michael Porter's Five Forces in your case question doesn't mean you did not get the answer right!

Additionally, this candidate makes an effort to think out loud so that the interviewer is fully aware of her thought process. This—along with frequent summaries of what she has learned so far and the direction she plans to take the discussion next—makes the case easy for the interviewer to follow and evaluate.

Business Strategy Case Questions

CASE 8

Your client is an operator of 20 restaurants in a medium-sized metropolitan city. Currently, it serves only lunch and dinner. It is thinking of expanding its offerings to include breakfast as well. What would you advise your client to do?

This is a typical strategy question that focuses on industry attractiveness and market entry strategy. It would be appropriate for undergrads or grad students. It also deals with restaurants, which everyone understands.

Bad Answer

Breakfasts are cheaper than lunch and dinner, so they're not as profitable. Also, who actually sits down for breakfast anymore? I usually just grab a bagel.

Where's the structure? Where's the analysis? Where's the framework? Where's the door?

Good Answer

Candidate: Hmmm, interesting issue. Let me take a couple of seconds to write down my thoughts.

It's okay to take some time to yourself to gather your thoughts. Be aware, though, that the interviewer may be watching what you write down to make sure that you're actually thinking about structure and content, and not just scribbling some random notes in an attempt to buy yourself some time. Also, don't take too long—the interviewer will start to become uncomfortable after about a minute or two.

Candidate: Okay, let me share how I'm going to structure this question. I look at this as a market entry question, so basically I need to evaluate how attractive the breakfast market is, and, if it is attractive, determine whether or not my client can execute profitably. At the risk of being overly structured, I'm going to ask you about the 4Cs, and then add a fifth one—capabilities—at the very end. My initial hypothesis is that the breakfast market is not attractive for my client because of the competitive environment, but I want to challenge this hypothesis as we go through the case.

It's difficult to be overly structured in a case interview. The candidate has done a good job of articulating how he is going to address the problem. Also, the candidate has generated a hypothesis that he wants to test; consultants appreciate hypothesis-driven candidates.

Candidate: Let me first ask you about the consumer. What sort of consumer does the restaurant target, and what are the key dynamics of that consumer?

Interviewer: To answer your first question, the client targets the time-starved, middle-income family who desires a healthy alternative to fast food. I'm not sure I understand what you mean by the second question.

Most likely, the interviewer knows exactly what you're looking for, but just wants you to elaborate so you can demonstrate that you know what you're talking about when you refer to consumer dynamics.

Candidate: What I'm looking for is basic consumer information: How often do they visit the restaurant? How much time do they spend at the restaurant? How does this compare with the industry average? Are there any differences between consumers among the 20 restaurants?

Any time you can ask about information to segment consumers, do so. Consultants love to talk about consumer segmentation.

Interviewer: Got it. Let me answer the last question first. There are actually some key differences between consumers by restaurant. Even though the client seeks to attract families, the locations of the restaurants have actually attracted a varied customer base. For example, six of the restaurants attract a business crowd, six of the restaurants attract a college student crowd, and the remaining eight restaurants attract the core consumer, the middle-income family. What are the insights that you would glean from this?

Candidate: I would imagine that breakfast at a restaurant would be of differing value to these various segments. For example, for the time-starved family, going to a restaurant for breakfast would probably not be very attractive because it would likely be faster to make something at home than to put the kids in the car and travel to a restaurant. In addition, making breakfast is not as involved as either lunch or dinner, so the time saving proposition would not be as compelling. So I would say, from a consumer perspective, it wouldn't make a lot of sense to offer breakfast at those six locations that attract families.

A simple but very logical explanation. Note also how the candidate drove to a conclusion quickly.

Candidate: For the business crowd, however, I would imagine it's a different story. Breakfast meetings remain important, so on the surface, it would appear that this might be an attractive opportunity. But I would need to know some more, both about the competition and the channel that the restaurant competes in, to make an informed decision.

The candidate has done a fine job of transitioning to a discussion around two of the other Cs: competition and channel.

Interviewer: First of all, let me tell you about the channel in which the restaurant competes. The restaurant is a quick-service format that is positioned between fast food options and casual restaurants such as TGI Fridays. Think of something like Panera Bread Company: Customers order and pay up front, and then bring their food to the table after receiving it from the counter.

Candidate: Hmmm, this doesn't seem like a great place for a breakfast meeting, where I imagine the focus is less on the food and more on having a relaxed place to be served and talk business.

Interviewer: That's true, but not all businesspeople have breakfast meetings. Could our client carve out a niche for the businessperson who wants a quick, healthy alternative to a donut shop or a bagel store?

Candidate: Is that what the competition is currently limited to: donut shops and bagel stores? What about a place to get a fruit salad or an egg sandwich?

Interviewer: Surprisingly, yes. There are not a lot of healthy options available nearby. And, from the client's own research, we know that there is an unmet need among business people for an alternative breakfast option.

Candidate: Well, it sounds like this could be an attractive option for the client. I want to talk about whether or not we can fill this gap profitably in a second, but first let's talk about the last consumer segment, the college students.

The candidate does an excellent job of controlling the discussion.

Candidate: Finally, we have the restaurants that attract the student crowd.

Interviewer: And do you believe that this segment would value a healthy breakfast option?

Candidate: What other alternatives do the students have?

Interviewer: Most of the students currently have a meal plan.

Candidate: And are they satisfied with their meal plans?

Interviewer: We do know that answer. But before I give it to you, how do you think you would go about getting the data?

Consultants can typically buy—or commission—research these days. But often, brute force reconnaissance is the way to go, and junior consultants often perform this type of work. The interviewer is asking you how you might go about your brute force.

Candidate: One option would be to go out and survey college students. Another possible source of data would be to look at the percent of students with meal plans over the last several years.

Interviewer: Yes, both are viable options. In fact, the student newspaper recently published a survey that said that most students are happy with the food service at the university.

Candidate: Well, this doesn't bode well for the client. If most students have meal plans, and most are happy with the service that is being provided, then students—who don't have a lot of extra cash—aren't likely to go to a restaurant for breakfast. I imagine they have better things to spend their money on.

Let's assume that the candidate means items such as books and presents for their significant others.

Interviewer: So, summarize where we are.

Candidate: Well, we've determined that the only viable option for the client is to serve breakfast at the six restaurants that attract the business consumer. What we haven't determined is whether the client can do it profitably or not.

Interviewer: And how would you go about doing this?

Candidate: We would need to conduct a basic profitability analysis by calculating both the revenues and costs of providing breakfast. First, let's look at the revenues.

Interviewer: And specifically how would you collect this data?

Candidate: One option would be to examine competitive information. There are likely restaurants outside our metropolitan area that are providing the same type of breakfast offering that our client would provide. I would travel to those locations and do some reconnaissance around what consumers are ordering and how much they are paying for it.

Interviewer: Agreed. Can you make a guess at what the typical order size is?

The interviewer is testing the candidate's ability to make a reasonable assumption. Consultants rarely have all the data, and therefore making assumptions becomes an important skill to learn.

Candidate: Well, given what we've said about the client's overall offering—that it's a healthy alternative to fast food—I'm going to guess that the overall price is going to be a little higher, but still fairly affordable. And let's say that the average order includes an egg sandwich, a fruit cup, and a small drink. If the egg sandwich and the fruit cup cost $3 each and the drink costs $1.50, then the average order size is $7.50.

Interviewer: And do you think that people are going to spend $7.50 on breakfast?

Candidate: That does sound high.

Interviewer: So, how would you modify your answer?

Candidate: I probably overestimated the amount of food that is consumed. It's more likely that the customer will have either an egg sandwich or a fruit cup—but not both—so the average would be about $4.50.

Interviewer: Let's assume that you're right. Let's also assume that the cost of this breakfast—ignoring for the moment the fact that the cost of the fruit is higher than the cost of the egg sandwich—is $3.50. Is this enough to make your decision?

As a matter of course, if the interviewer asks you "is this enough," the answer will be no. In this case, the interviewer is doing some of the cost analysis for you, but leaving out a key component.

Candidate: The cost of the food is not the only cost to be considered. We also must factor in labor costs.

Interviewer: Right. But we cannot allocate a specific labor cost to the egg sandwich or the drink. So how do you incorporate labor costs into your equation?

Candidate: One way to look at it would be to do the cost/benefit analysis for an entire breakfast period. So, for example, let's assume the following: the restaurant is open from 6 a.m. to 10 a.m. for breakfast. The restaurant needs five people to prepare, serve, clean, and manage the registers. This equates to 20 hours total. Let's say that the client pays the employees $8 per hour, or $160 per breakfast shift. Earlier, we concluded that each transaction yields $1 in profit; that is, the $4.50 revenue minus the $3.50 in costs. So the break-even point is 160 transactions.

The candidate shows facility with making assumptions. The interviewer will be looking less at the quality of those assumptions and more at where you are choosing to make assumptions. In this example, the candidate has made assumptions that lead him to a logical—and insightful—conclusion.

Interviewer: And do you think that 160 is reasonable?

Candidate: Again, let's think about this on a per shift basis. 160 transactions in 4 hours is 40 transactions per hour, or a little less than one a minute. This seems to me pretty challenging, particularly if the restaurant is going to serve anything hot.

Interviewer: I agree. So what do you think the client could do to make this profitable?

Candidate: One option would be to examine the staffing levels: Do you need five people? Another option would be to focus solely on preprepared food such as fruit salads. This may allow you to reach the 40 transactions per hour.

Well done. The candidate did a good job of bringing structure to the case, following prompts, and generating options. Note that the candidate never got to the capability discussion; oftentimes in cases, the flow of the discussion will not lead logically to where you might imagine it at the beginning. This is natural—and expected. Just be prepared to go with the flow.

CASE 9

You have just been hired by Pluto, a candy company with a long tradition of making chocolaty treats. You have joined a 6-month old division that has been tasked with diversifying the company's product offerings by developing a new candy product that is not chocolate-based. You have been hired as a business analyst reporting to the lead product manager on this new product—but the exact product has not yet been conceived, named, or launched. What would you want to know in order to supply your team with the right information to determine what product your new division should make? How would you get that information?

This is a case focused on a classic strategy problem—one similar to any number of business strategy problems you would be likely to face on a typical management consulting project or within many types of manufacturing and marketing organizations in a competitive marketplace. There are one or two pieces of important information that the candidate should be able to infer from the interviewer's setup of the case problem. However, most of the information the candidate would need to properly analyze the strategy issues at play here require further probing on the part of the candidate. This case therefore tests the candidate on both her ability to acquire the proper information to identify the nature of the business strategy problem at hand, and her ability to develop one or more potential solutions to the strategy problem and communicate them as options (rather than answers) for the interviewer to consider. For purposes of simplicity on strategy case questions like these, think of them as having two parts: half information discovery and synthesis, and half analysis and development of recommendations.

Bad Answers

- Well, I would spend some time in the candy aisles and figure out what other types of candy seem to be doing well. It seems to me that hard candies that taste like fruits are a big part of the candy selection in stores these days, so I'd probably start by recommending that we do some testing of fruit flavors and see if we can find a delicious one that we could give a cool new name and some fun flashy packaging.

In most strategy case interview situations, you will NOT have enough at the outset to even begin to provide a recommendation or your ideas. Instead, always consider the many areas you could or would investigate to gather more information before jumping to conclusions or answers to the case problem before even considering sharing a potential recommendation about what to do. Answers like this demonstrate that the candidate thinks she knows enough to handle any business problem right away, no matter how foreign the problem is to her experience. This not only belies a quick-to-judge attitude based on opinions rather than customer and marketplace data—which is a red flag for any savvy employer—but it shortchanges the candidate AND the interviewer.

- I'm not so interested in the candy industry. As my cover letter to your company indicated, I'm really interested in working in software, so I'm not sure I'd have very good ideas about how to help a candy company where I'm never going to work anyway. Can we talk about an example of a problem that a technology company might have? I know lots about how to deal with problems in the software and technology industry.

Even if you have indicated a preference for a different kind of role or industry, this is NOT the time to reinforce what you are and are not interested in doing. These cases allow the interviewer to gain insight into the candidate's general knowledge and application of generic business strategy principles. Microsoft was once famous (perhaps overly so) for incorporating case questions in interviews that had puzzles, math, logic problems, and wildly different industry issues and business challenges from their own industry. The purpose, of course, was to see how a candidate thought about different problems and, secondarily, how they handled themselves under the pressure of an unexpected question. Be prepared to share your thinking, rather than provide an answer . . . and certainly don't decline to address an interview question because you don't care for it.

- Why are they even thinking of straying from their tried-and-true formula of chocolate candies at all? I think one of the first things I would want to do is to try all of the candies that they already produce and just make sure they aren't missing the boat with a big opportunity on a candy that they already make.

A strong candidate keeps her options open in the first half of the case—through information discovery and consideration. Don't lead by taking the case in a totally different direction from the one setup in the opening of the discussion. If you are told there is a new division with a new product mandate, don't second-guess the theoretical company managers unless you've discovered enough information to make you quite confident that the setup is worth questioning. Instead, assume that the setup was provided to help you get started and begin moving forward with probing questions and a discussion of the situation with your interviewer.

Good Answer

Candidate: An interesting situation, and one I can imagine a talented new marketing graduate getting thrown into since companies often like to have fresh ideas and fresh approaches applied to new products. Before I begin thinking about how I might respond to the request for a recommendation on this issue, I need to learn more information first. So I can understand the nature of the marketplace and competition, can you tell me if the market for nonchocolate candies is expanding or contracting right now? And how are Pluto's competitors doing with their nonchocolate candies currently on the market?

Good start. The candidate has acknowledged that she will need to learn and consider more information before being ready to make a recommendation, which is the key first step in any strategy project—get the data! The candidate has chosen a big picture inquiry to start the investigation and data gathering—an assessment of the health of the overall market demand for the types of products that Pluto is considering, with a request for more information about the relative fortunes and performance of other candy makers as a proxy and directional indicator if the market has promise for Pluto at all.

Interviewer: Good question. Yes, Pluto's competitors have all found success with different product extensions in consumer candies that are not chocolate. All of these products are doing quite well—in fact, whereas 5 years ago there were only ten nonchocolate candies on the store shelves, now there are more than 25 different choices. Only two newly introduced nonchocolate candy products from competitors have failed during this time.

Good information has been provided here, even more than the candidate was seeking. This is often the case with strategy case interviews—the interviewer will generally guide and provide information to the candidate when it is intelligently and respectfully requested.

Candidate: Interesting—it sounds like consumer demand for these kinds of candies is strong, given the growth in the general product category. And from the sound of things, consumers are trying many different types of these candies since only two have failed to find sufficient demand to stay in market while 15 have had enough demand to remain in the market. Was there a common factor to the two candies that failed?

The candidate shows a good connection between market demand and supply—when supply to the marketplace is expanding, it is usually indicative of a competitive market with healthy product demand that has either been unmet in the past or is currently expanding. This is a good sign for Pluto.

Interviewer: Yes, both of the candies that failed were hard candies based on mint flavors, whereas all of the successful new candy products have been soft or chewy fruit flavored candies.

Hmmm. The interviewer is really providing a lot of information here. Sometimes a candidate will get rewarded in this way for good questioning and provided with information that can come in handy in investigating the case.

Candidate: Interesting. I'll keep that in mind later as I'm narrowing in on the potential product ideas. For now though, I want to stay focused on the task at hand for me to be most useful in my role on the team, which is investigating the market opportunity and supplying some direction as to what new product we should build and launch. The first thing I would want to do is to arm myself with as much quantitative and qualitative data as I could. I would want to collect any market research already available within or outside the company, as well as get my hands on unit sales and market demand data for the industry and from competitors' products if it's publicly available. Do you know if there are industry publications or trade associations that publish sales and marketing data like this?

Interviewer: Good thinking. Yes, there is a lot of great data available about unit sales volumes by product type. Some of it is within Pluto, but some would require a little research and work to dig up. Where would you look to get it?

The interviewer remains pretty tough here and is communicating that he wants to hear how you would do market and demand research—a very common task of business analysts and marketing professionals working on consumer products and services.

Candidate: Well, as I mentioned, I would collect and summarize analyst reports, review relevant trade industry articles recently published that discuss market demand for these types of products, collect and review any other historical research done within Pluto, and make use of the Internet and industry associations for more public information. If there were a research budget or an easy means of collecting customer opinions—perhaps through Pluto's website or PR and advertising firms—I would do some short-term or low-cost primary research to understand the customer needs with regard to nonchocolate candy products as well. Depending on the budget and time frames, I could even do some focus group research and test consumer attitudes about a variety of different nonchocolate candies on the market. Finally, I recall from my econometrics class that quantitative surveys offer the ability to measure the relative appeal of different characteristics for similar products. All of this kind of research would be helpful in building up my analysis of the potential directions we could go with our new product.

Interviewer: All of those sound like good sources of information. If the product manager told you that she was focused on fruit flavors for the new product, how would you pick a particular flavor to recommend?

Now the interviewer is focusing the candidate's thinking on a specific problem: which flavor to choose. The goal is to see how a candidate thinks about a bounded, specific problem with a finite number of possible outcomes.

Candidate: Well, the first piece of data I'd want to collect and review would be the flavors already available on the market. I'd like to know the number of instances as well as which flavors of candies are already successful in the market—as that would give some sense of relative demand as well as yield clues as to potential new fruit flavors that are similar to—but not the exact same as—some of the more successful flavors. Also, I'd like to collect some data from the domestic grocery stores about volume of sales of actual fruit. That would be a good indicator of the appeal—and potential market—of specific fruit flavors here within this U.S. market. Finally, I'd be interested in reviewing the results of my primary research—assuming I had the time to conduct surveys and focus group research and the like—to analyze the demand for certain fruit flavors and extrapolate out to determine which ones had the largest market opportunity according to our own research.

Well done. The candidate listed at least two or three solid sources of data, including both qualitative and quantitative ones. This is usually a sufficient list size when an interviewer asks you to provide a potential list in a response. The candidate has also demonstrated a key skill: using the data to build up a projection of overall market demand—and therefore business opportunity—for the new product.

Interviewer: That sounds like a good list of potential sources of data. In a basic sense, how would you choose which flavor to ultimately recommend to your team for the new product?

Here the interviewer wants to hear specifics of the candidate's application of the SWOT framework (Strengths, Weaknesses, Opportunities, Threats) to a business opportunity—in this case, a framework to support a particular recommendation, no matter what that recommendation is.

Candidate: I would want to recommend a flavor that I believed had the biggest currently unmet market opportunity. In other words, the flavor that had the biggest difference between the relative ranking of the flavor's appeal in the market according to my research and its current presence in the market in other competitors' products. The reason that I would suggest this approach is that it presents the biggest potential opportunity for a new product in an already competitive market—since there is no existing threat of competition until after our product flavor launches and becomes successful. With no entrenched products which already have a brand presence in a particular fruit flavor, the relative lack of threats to our new product means that we might have an easier time establishing a new brand and slot in a growing product category than if we just issued another variation on an existing flavor.

The candidate has presented a good foundation for her suggestion: Rather than intuition or opinion, she has used a more quantitative and analytical basis for her answer. There could have been other answers here, but the best ones will use some reference to the research and analysis as the basis for the recommendation.

Interviewer: That sounds like a good approach. What if I told you that berry flavors were extremely appealing to the American public, but not represented in the marketplace for nonchocolate candies yet? Let's assume that your analysis shows the same: The market opportunity is the largest for berry candies. How would you decide whether to introduce a single candy with one type of berry flavor, multiple candy products with different berry flavors, a single product with one flavor that is an invented blend of many berry flavors, or a single product with multiple berry flavors offered all in one package?

Here the interviewer has given good feedback and support to the candidate for the analytical basis that the candidate has suggested, but has not let the candidate get off easy. The candidate will have to provide some additional evidence of her analytical and market-sizing skills.

Candidate: That's an interesting problem to face. A couple of questions, so that I can think about this a little more thoroughly: First, is there only enough investment or production capacity allocated by the company for one product? Second, can you tell me if the research on berry flavors as the largest category of unmet consumer demand shows one particular berry way out in front of all the others, or are there several berry flavors all with different market opportunity but similar in distinct market appeal?

The candidate has taken a wise tack here: She has chosen to consider the question; and, having determined that she might need more information in order to answer the interviewer's question as effectively as possible, she has asked a few follow-up questions. This is positive, a sign of patience coupled with action on the candidate's part—the right balance of thinking skills for a successful business strategist. Candidates should know that it's okay to ask for more data when needed—just so long as they don't turn the interview into a never-ending loop of questions without ever using the responses to formulate an answer.

Interviewer: Good questions. First, the company is only willing to allocate enough of the production plant to produce one new candy product, so you must pick just one option. Second, as it turns out, your research shows that strawberries, raspberries, and blueberries are all equally appealing to the American consumer—and then there is a gap between the appeal of those berries and the remainder.

Okay, now the candidate should know enough to be able to wrap up her answer to the question.

Candidate: Well, given what you've told me, I would then suggest the last option you presented—the introduction of a candy that contains three distinct berry flavors with those three flavors offered and described on the candy packaging. This way, we would be targeting the aggregated total potential market audience of new customers out there who prefer at least one of the three berry flavors we are offering, without necessarily sacrificing the opportunity to reach the other two. I believe that with good marketing and packaging, this would give us the largest potential market and therefore likelihood of success for our new product out of the choices available.

This is a great answer. It incorporates one of the choices presented by the interviewer, it uses the information provided by the case in a logical way, and it matches classical business theory about targeting the largest possible unmet market with a new product.

Interviewer: Good idea—I'm sure that Pluto will take your suggestion. If the product were introduced and were proven to be a wild success, what additional research would you want to do in order to determine if line extensions or product spin-offs are possible to increase the potential of this new product line for Pluto?

Candidate: Probably the key piece of information I'd like to research would be whether one particular berry flavor of the three in our new candy is more appealing to the typical buyer than the other ones. Additionally, I'd like to review the store sales data and customer focus group research to determine if unit volumes sold were due to single purchases or repeat purchases by the same people. If we were to find that one flavor was driving more than one-third of the repeat sales of our new candy and we found that purchasers of our new candy were loyal enough to buy it numerous times, then we might be able to spin off a new candy product featuring only that one flavor that was most appealing to the core target audience for our original product. Alternatively, if we found that our research pointed in a slightly different direction, we could introduce an additional new product or two that incorporates the same format and branding, but substitutes in slightly different combinations of three flavors. Either of these would allow us to "test the waters" of adding new customers and market opportunity with a small variation on an existing successful product, which is less risky than starting from scratch with an entirely new product, brand, etc.

Interviewer: Interesting ideas. Let's hope that your first product does well enough that the company's managers encourage you to replicate its success with additional products. Thanks for your time—I've appreciated hearing your approach to this new product opportunity.

Well done. It sounds like the interviewer has heard enough of the candidate's thinking on this case to be satisfied with the progress made and comfortable that she has employed a strong enough approach to wrap up this particular case.

CASE 10

Your client is a major pharmaceutical company whose research and development department has developed a promising new drug compound, but is uncertain as to what to do with it. Should it license its brand or manage the entry in-house?

This is a common new markets/expansion strategy question. However, the licensing element (a "launch vs sell" strategy question rather than a more typical "make vs buy" investment decision) presents an interesting challenge.

Bad Answer

They should absolutely build and launch the drug themselves. There is no way they can get paid enough if they license it to someone else compared to what they can make if they launch it and keep all the profits for themselves.

This is a one-line answer to a question that must have some complexity to it, or else what is the point in asking it in the first place? Shutting down the case so quickly with your "answer" doesn't allow the interviewer the opportunity to see how you think.

Good Answer

Candidate: This is an interesting one. I can't say I'm too familiar with the pharmaceutical industry, but I'm sure I can ask some questions along the way to sort through the issues. This case hinges on the costs and benefits of licensing the new drug compound versus the costs and benefits of developing the new drug in-house. Comparing the two is interesting because licensing the drug would provide an immediate revenue stream as well as the potential for future payments, while the "build and launch" option would have higher up-front costs and longer time to receive any revenue—but potentially a larger payout in the long run. Therefore, it seems that my first step should be to weigh the relative economics of licensing versus the in-house scenario, and determine which one has the larger net present value (NPV) in terms of current and future profitability for the company. So that I can understand the first scenario a little better, could you please give me a sense for how a licensing arrangement would work financially? Is there a potential licensee already lined up, and if so what do the economics look like so far?

Good start. The candidate has clearly spelled out his approach to the case, and has started with the big picture. In addition, he's not afraid to ask a question about licensing arrangements, a very specific area with which he's not familiar. It's always better to ask the question than to pretend you know things that you don't. Finally, he has clearly spelled out his criteria for judging which option to choose: He will select the option that is likely to provide the highest NPV profits to the company, which is a solid criterion for business strategy decision making.

Interviewer: In a licensing scenario, the client would choose a competing pharma company with the best bid—or deal terms—for licensing and marketing the new drug. From a financial standpoint, the client would collect $125 million in up-front licensing fees, plus 10 percent royalty on gross revenue of the product for the first 5 years that it is in the market.

Great. The candidate got what he needed—he just needs to know a little more to understand what the NPV of the licensing opportunity is potentially worth.

Candidate: Thank you; that's helpful. I just need to know one more thing about the licensing option: What is the length of time that our client believes its competitor will require in order to get this drug to market and launched?

The data hunt continues.

Interviewer: If your client licensed this drug compound to one of the leading producers of over-the-counter drugs in the market, they could get it launched and in market 2 years after FDA approval, which typically takes about 5 years.

The interviewer has provided good information here. In addition to answering the candidate's question, she also provided another key piece of data: the length of time any drug producer, whether it is the client or a licensee, would require to get through drug FDA approval.

Candidate: Okay, that's interesting to know. I need to learn a little more to make my decision in this case. What is the expected market for this product? Can you give me a sense for the potential size of this drug market in terms of annual sales? And is there a discount rate that I should apply to calculating the present value of those future payments from the sales of the drug?

The candidate is still driving through the fact-gathering stage.

Interviewer: You can assume that the annual market for this drug would be approximately 10 million units. You can also assume that the market will bear a price of $2 per unit. As for discount rate, I'm impressed that you know how to calculate a NPV, and I'm sure that it would be used for a sophisticated ROI analysis like this, but for the purposes of this case just assume 0 percent so that your NPV analysis only involves simple math. Sound fair?

So, this data is all providing the components needed to get to a decision based on good numbers and solid analytics. In this case, the interviewer made it slightly easier on the candidate by not requiring him to go to the calculator to actually compute the multiplication of a real NPV analysis.

Candidate: Okay, one last question for you: If the client retained that drug for an in-house production and marketing plan, how long would it take to get to market and what would it cost the company to do so? Also, how long would it earn its revenues from the drug once it launched it?

Good. The candidate is driving to calculate the other side of this NPV in order to compare the numbers and make the decision—good analytical reasoning and decision making requires all the numbers.

Interviewer: Good question. If the client does the work itself, it anticipates costs of $30 million to get the drug ready for trials and then to market. It could expect the same 5 years to get the drug through FDA trials, but because it's not as adept at marketing and launching products as its rivals, it thinks it would take 4 more years to get the product in market. Once in market, the company can reasonably expect it to have 10 solid years of sales before other market entrants cannibalize its profits and its market opportunity dries up due to generic entry. For the purposes of this case, assume that once the drug is in market, it costs $5 million a year to produce and market it.

The interviewer has made the calculations a little easier for the candidate by eliminating annual costs from the equation. Now the candidate has collected all the information he needs to compare the numbers and provide an answer. In the interest of completeness and openness though, it's always best for the candidate to do his thinking out loud to show his facility with numbers and analytics. This is an appealing function to interviewers who meet lots of candidates who are eager, but few who can really run the numbers with great facility.

Candidate: Okay, so now I believe I know what I need in order to make a good decision about what the client should do. From the information you've provided me, and based on the lack of a discount rate assumption for the NPV calculation, I estimate that the licensing option is worth $100 million + 10 percent of $20 million x 5 years, or an additional $10 million. This equates to a total of $110 million in net value to the client, with no costs.

Interviewer: Good, that's my estimate too for that option. Go on . . .

A good validation that the candidate is driving to a good answer.

Candidate: So, based on what you've said, the new drug would be worth 10 years of $20 million a year, so $200 million in total revenue. On the cost side, however, the company would require $30 million to get to market plus $5 million a year for 10 years to keep producing it in market to earn its revenue. That's a total of $80 million in costs. The net profits to the client if it launched the product itself would be $120 million. However, they would have to wait 2 more years to start earning their profits.

Good work—solid math and a chance to finally answer the question.

Interviewer: Okay, that sounds like solid analysis. So what is your recommendation to the client?

Here, the interviewer seems to validate much of the candidate's approach, and wants the candidate to wrap up his analysis.

Candidate: Well, just looking at the numbers and with the simple assumption that we've made about no discount rate to reduce back the present value of the future payment streams which will accrue to this company, it appears that keeping the drug in-house and producing it themselves will be $10 million more profitable to this client in the long term.

Good—a solid answer based on real numbers. But the interviewer has space to challenge the candidate to consider other options, and may do so.

Interviewer: Good—but what are some of the other, nonquantitative elements of this case that you might also want to know before you provided a final recommendation to the client?

Candidate: Well, although the in-house option appears to pay out better for the client than licensing in the long term, there are a few other things to consider. One, is there any risk of failure of the drug in the marketplace, and the drug not earning the expected market opportunity in terms of total units sold per year? If there is, then the up-front payment from licensing might be a much more appealing route, since it is money in hand and it isn't dependent on the future success of the product since another company then owns the future opportunity and only the subsequent revenue share is risk-bearing for the client. Also, the client should consider the possible risk of the new product failing while in FDA trials—again, if there is nonzero risk of this happening, then it raises the appeal of the licensing option versus building the drug in-house, since the risk is on the licensee's shoulders to steward the drug successfully through FDA approval and to market. Finally, operational and marketing competencies should be considered. If the client is simply an R&D shop, and has never actually produced and marketed a new drug successfully, then it might have a risk of complete failure and never be able to actually get the drug out and earning positive revenues for itself—or do so with substantially higher costs than it currently anticipates to get it done. All of these are risks or unknowns that could potentially swing the economics of the case in favor of a licensing choice—if we were to learn that they were relevant and impactful.

Great work. The candidate provided a solid overview of a few of the other considerations that could net down the actual expected value of the client's in-house production option and net up the licensing option value to the client.

Interviewer: Sounds good. I think that's a solid overview of some of the other key considerations we would need to explore with this client before we made a recommendation based solely on the numbers. Good work.

CASE 11

Your client is the vice president of marketing for a major cosmetic company. He is considering whether or not to introduce a line of men's cologne for Wal-Mart. What are the major issues he should be thinking about?

Unlike the prior two strategy cases, this case is more focused on identifying the types of analyses and questions that you—as a consultant—would need to ask and answer. Sometimes interviewers will give candidates two small cases in one interview; this is an example of a shorter case that may be asked in that situation.

Bad Answer

Probably not a good idea. Perfume is a luxury product that is probably not a big seller for Wal-Mart because the Wal-Mart consumer does not value high-end products.

This is a complete dud answer, and the interviewer will be wondering if it's even worth her while to continue.

Good Answer

Candidate: Okay. Let me organize my answers around the 4Cs: consumer, channel, cost, and competition.

Interviewer: I've heard of the 4Cs before. Let's start with consumer: What are the key consumer dynamics that you would look for?

Candidate: A couple of things pop to mind. First of all, I'd want to know the market size of cologne at Wal-Mart, both in terms of revenue and units sold. This will give me a general sense of the consumers' interest in cologne, as well as how much he is willing to pay for a bottle. In addition, I'd want to know the growth rates—and how the growth rates compare to other channels, such as department stores.

Interviewer: And anything besides the market data?

As in other cases in this guide—and in all cases when you're interviewing—the answer is going to be yes.

Candidate: Yes. For example, I'd want to know why men are buying more (or less) cologne. Are there certain segments of the population (for example, younger men) that comprise most of the sales? Maybe it's women buying men's cologne—I'd want to get all the data I could about the specific buyer and the occasion for which she is buying.

Interviewer: Why would the specific buyer matter? Wouldn't the market-size data give you all that you need?

Candidate: Well, we need to consider marketing messaging and packaging as well. If the consumer is an older man the packaging of the cologne is going to be different than if the consumer is a younger woman.

Good point. Score one for the candidate.

Interviewer: Let's move on to the channel dynamics.

Candidate: Well, we already talked a little about the channel dynamics when I mentioned how I'd want to assess the different growth rates in cologne between department stores and Wal-Mart. In addition to this analysis, I would want to do a strategic assessment on the health of the channel as a whole.

Interviewer: What sort of analyses would you perform to drive to an answer?

Candidate: I would do work to assess whether or not expansion into cologne—or beauty products in general—is a strategic priority for Wal-Mart. If it is, then the client can be sure that Wal-Mart is making a commitment to its product; if Wal-Mart is going in a different direction, then I would advise the client to think carefully about making an investment in Wal-Mart.

Interviewer: And what about the economic and supply pressures that Wal-Mart places on its suppliers? Do you think this would be an important issue to consider in your channel analysis?

Candidate: Absolutely! I was going to address this when I got to the cost section, as the economic considerations are incredibly important. For example, what are the margins that Wal-Mart requires? Does the client have the cost structure to support these margins and still make money? What does the client's balance sheet look like? Does it have the working capital to support the inventory requirements to serve a big retailer such as Wal-Mart?

The candidate does a nice job of being fluid between the Cs. Though the Cs are a nice organizing principle, they frequently overlap, as the candidate demonstrates here.

Interviewer: What other sort of cost issues would you look into?

Candidate: Again, I'm going to blend the channel analysis with the cost analysis, but I'd want to look at the relative profitability across channels.

Interviewer: And how would you do this?

Candidate: One way to do it would be to compare an existing product against a hypothetical product for Wal-Mart. I could look at the P&L statement for the existing product and then create a hypothetical P&L for the new product.

Interviewer: And where would you expect to see the major differences?

The interviewer is taking the candidate away from the Cs for a second.

Candidate: The wholesale price would be different, but hopefully lower costs and higher units would make up the difference.

Interviewer: One would hope. Now let's go on to competition. What would you want to know here?

Candidate: The first thing I'd do is look at the current competitive set: Who is serving Wal-Mart now, and how are they positioning themselves? I'd look for any data that would allow me to see if they've been successful, such as new product additions, expanded shelf space, or very compelling financial results. What I'd also want to do is look at who might be the client's competition in the future. Are there other players who might try to enter the business at Wal-Mart? What are their relative strengths and weaknesses? How could the client position itself against them? And finally, I'd want to know how the competitors in my current distribution channels might act if the client were to go to Wal-Mart. Would they follow? Would they step up their marketing and sales activities in the current channels in order to try to steal share, assuming that the client is preoccupied with the entry into Wal-Mart? There would be a lot of interesting game theory questions that would need to be answered.

Interviewer: Thanks for your thoughts. Now let's move on to a resume question.

Resume Case Questions

CASE 12

Talk to me about a business leader for whom you have a lot of respect.

Often, so-called resume questions will not focus specifically on your resume; rather, they will delve into why you want to go into the business world and how intelligently you can speak about business issues that are not spelled out on your resume.

Bad Answer

Candidate: Donald Trump, Bill Gates, the founders of Google. They've all made a ton of money and live a celebrity lifestyle.

The interviewer will quickly determine that you are not fit to live the consulting lifestyle.

Good Answer

Candidate: Someone I really respect is Howard Schultz at Starbucks. He combines qualities that I really admire in a business leader: vision, execution, innovation, and social responsibility. Also, since I get my venti nonfat, no-foam, extra-hot latte every morning from the local Starbucks, I can't imagine life without what he's created.

The candidate does a nice job of structuring her response by clearly identifying why she admires Howard Schultz. The interviewer may be wondering about the complicated beverage choice, but that should not affect the interview decision!

Candidate: Let's first talk about the vision thing. Ten years ago, who would have thought that people would pay $5 for a coffee drink? He had an insight—that he wanted to bring the atmosphere of the Italian coffee house to the United States—and doggedly pursued it despite major market trends that were not in his favor.

Interviewer: So do you believe that strong business leaders should ignore business trends?

Note how the interviewer is using what the candidate said to test how she looks at and interprets data.

Candidate: Certainly not. Clearly analyzing the major market forces, for example using the 4Cs, is essential to business success. What Mr. Schultz did was to draw a different conclusion from the data. And that was that, though the retail price of coffee was declining, no one had tried to make a major change in the quality of the coffee and, more importantly, the experience of drinking it. And he saw that as an opportunity.

The candidate has done a fantastic job of responding to the interviewer's challenge: She answered the question (even throwing in a gratuitous framework!) and demonstrated the importance of teasing out new insight from widely available data.

Candidate: Which leads me to my second point around execution. Mr. Schultz made several smart decisions along the way, which, in my opinion, have been critical to his success.

Interviewer: Tell me about the decision you consider to be most important.

Candidate: I think that tightly managing the Starbucks experience by not pursuing a franchise model was a wise decision. With the rapid expansion of the retail operations, it would have been very easy to Mr. Schultz to create a franchise network. However, he realized that the Starbucks experience is as important as the product itself, and therefore that controlling the store environment is essential. The consumer wants the same look and feel regardless of where he or she shops, and Mr. Schultz believed he could better satisfy that need if he controlled the network.

The candidate provides a nice summary of the pros and cons of the decision.

Interviewer: OK. You also mentioned innovation. Tell me a little more about why you consider Starbucks innovative.

Candidate: They have done an excellent job of moving beyond just service coffee, but have done so in a way that has both leveraged and enhanced the brand. Let's take music. As you know, you can buy CDs at Starbucks. What music has to do with coffee, I'm not sure. But the Starbucks brand represents serenity and comfort, and that is the type of music that is offered. I recently purchased a Nat King Cole CD at Starbucks. Would I have bought this at a record store? Probably not. But it seemed appropriate to buy at Starbucks. On the other hand, I'm not going to buy a Metallica CD at Starbucks, nor would they offer one—it doesn't mesh with the brand.

The candidate continues to do an excellent job of demonstrating understanding of the Starbucks business model and its consumer value proposition.

Also, note that the candidate has offered a personal experience. In general, be cautious about doing this. In this instance it works for two reasons: 1) It is relevant and serves to enhance the candidate's argument, and 2) this is a case question about personal preferences, so sharing personal experience is appropriate.

Candidate: And, finally, Mr. Schultz has used his success to give back to the community. And he has infused this sense of corporate responsibility into his company as well. Starbucks encourages and rewards volunteerism among its employees and has a strong track record of treating its suppliers and growers with equity.

What Mr. Schultz has done is show a combination of vision, smart execution decisions, innovation, and social responsibility. These are qualities that I would like to develop as I pursue a career in business.

An excellent summary.

Interviewer: Thank you for your time.

CASE 13

Tell me about a business trend that you're following closely.

Similar to the previous case, the interviewer is gauging the candidate's business acumen. In this case, it does not matter what you choose. What will be important here is that you speak with some knowledge and passion about a business trend. Consultants love to discuss and debate all sorts of industry trends and, if you're about to spend a lot of time with them, they'll need to know that you enjoy engaging in this sort of discussion.

Bad Answer

Candidate: I wish that I could spend time following the business press more, but with school and extracurricular activities, I'm finding myself swamped.

Though likely a true answer, this is not a sufficient one. You will need to be prepared to speak intelligently about one or two current events or trends.

Good Answer

Candidate: To be perfectly honest, I wish that I had more time to follow what's going on in the business world. However, over the last several months I've made the conscious decision to prioritize school and my leadership responsibilities in several extracurricular activities. This is not to say that I haven't been reading the *Journal* and *Business Week* on a somewhat regular basis, but I feel as if I'm doing this just to keep up with current events.

Note how much better this response is than the bad answer above. The candidate explains that he has made a conscious choice to focus on other areas and has nicely slipped in a plug about his leadership positions outside school. He also indicates that he is familiar with the major business publications.

Interviewer: I understand. But I'm going to press you on this one: Which of the current events is most interesting?

The interviewer is not letting the candidate off the hook.

Candidate: I recently read about Federated Department Stores acquiring May Department Stores, and the article discussed other consolidation in the retail industry. Having grown up in the Midwest and shopped stores owned by May most of my life, I found intriguing.

Interviewer: OK. But, from a business perspective, what do you think this acquisition means? Why do you think that Federated decided to buy May?

Clearly, the interviewer is not getting what she wants from the candidate. Don't panic: Particularly on resume questions, the cases can go in many directions. Just take a deep breath and push on; you will always get one chance to course correct. Also, note how weaving in personal experience in this question did not work (unlike the previous resume question).

Candidate: The article mentioned several reasons for the acquisition. First, Federated is seeking to expand its geographic territory, and the May Department Stores "footprint" is complementary. Second, there are scale advantages associated with being larger. And, third, Federated believes that it can add value by rolling out its strategy, which focuses on exclusive brands and labels, to May Department Stores.

The candidate summarizes the major deal points in a very concise and articulate way.

Interviewer: Which of these do you believe to be the most important?

A good interviewer will always ask the candidate for his or her own assessment of the situation, rather than allowing the candidate to rely on what the press is saying.

Candidate: I don't know a lot about the intricacies of Federated's strategy around exclusive brands and labels, so I'm not sure how to evaluate that one. So I would say that the scale advantages are most important. And let me tell you why.

The candidate has picked up on the interviewer's insistence for providing rationale for each answer.

Candidate: I think scale will play itself out here in two ways. One, I imagine that there will be some back-office savings in areas such as finance, customer service, and corporate administration. Where I see the more interesting benefits from scale, however, is in purchasing power. For example, it's likely that both Federated and May buy from Nike. But obviously they do so separately. A combined entity will have more power and potentially can ask for sharper pricing.

Interviewer: Can you think of another player in the industry that is doing this?

Candidate: Well, even though it may not be targeting the same consumer with the same product offering, Wal-Mart certainly has benefited from its size in terms of negotiating prices with its customers.

Another solid response. The candidate reveals that he has some sense of basic industry dynamics (that the department store consumer is different from the value consumer), but that the strategies (purchasing power) can be consistent across the different segments.

Interviewer: Good. It'll be interesting to see what happens in the retail world over the next 12 to 18 months. I enjoyed our discussion.

CASE 14

What other industries are you considering entering? Why is consulting your first choice?

This sort of question is more likely to be asked of a candidate who has a very focused resume (e.g., biotech/life sciences, financial services). Note how this question is also a thinly veiled effort to ask the candidate why he or she wants to go into consulting.

Bad Answer

Candidate: At this point, consulting is the only field I'm interested in. I think that the breadth of experiences is going to be worthwhile no matter where I ultimately end up.

Not a terrible answer, but you don't want to come across as putting all your eggs in the consulting basket. If consulting is your only choice, then you will need to explain proactively why you're narrowed your choices so much.

Good Answer

Candidate: I'm not surprised that you asked this question, as I've gotten something like it in most of my consulting interviews to date. The bottom line is that, even though my resume suggests that should go into public service, I believe that pursuing a career in consulting will allow me to develop a broad skill set that is applicable regardless of the industry I ultimately end up in.

The candidate gives an honest assessment of the situation and a concise summary answer. He recognizes the thrust of the question and also does a nice job of subtle self-promotion by referring to other consulting interviews.

Candidate: This is not to say that I am cutting off other options. Specifically, I've taken the LSAT and am applying to law school. Also, I'm pursuing jobs in the public sector. However, I've been highly selective in both these areas. I've only applied to the top three law schools and, if I get in, I will try to defer while I get some real-world work experience. Mainly, I've had time over the past semester to focus a lot of effort on my application process, and I'm afraid if I get a job and then decide to apply that I won't have the time to put in the effort required. My job search in the public sector has been very focused as well. I'm working through one of my professors who has great contacts in the Environmental Protection Agency to see if I can get a position there as a senior analyst.

There is some chance that the candidate could appear scattered by looking into consulting, law school, and the public sector. But he does present a strong case for why he has chosen to look at all three simultaneously.

Interviewer: And how did you make the decision to interview with consulting firms?

Candidate: It's interesting how I got here. At the beginning of the year, I thought that there was no way that I would interview with consulting firms. As you see from my resume, my coursework and summer internships have focused more on the environment and public policy issues than on economics and finance. And I've both excelled at and enjoyed what I've done. So I came into this year assuming that I would end up in Washington or in law school. Earlier this year, however, some friends dragged me to a consulting panel by saying that there were free cookies. And I was surprised at how much I enjoyed the presentation.

Interviewer: What specifically surprised you?

Candidate: Two things. The first was the diversity of experiences that consulting offers. One person talked about how she worked in Croatia for a shipping company one summer and then did a big technology M&A deal that fall. She spoke very enthusiastically about the different challenges that she faced to ensure that the projects were successful and the different skills that she developed.

Interviewer: Tell me more.

Candidate: Well, on the case in Croatia she said that what she learned was how to manage difficult clients and how she developed her influencing skills. On the M&A case, she mentioned the analytic and modeling skills that she learned. And, in both cases, she mentioned that there were colleagues there to help her develop the skills. While I was sitting there, I thought about how helpful these skills would have been to me in the internships I've had.

Interviewer: You mentioned something else besides the diversity of experience. What was that?

Candidate: What I didn't realize is that there is a possibility of doing some consulting to nonprofits as well. And certainly that is attractive to me.

Interviewer: That's true. Some firms, such as Bain, have even started their own non-profit consulting arms. But you do realize that most of the work we do is for for-profit companies.

Candidate: Of course. However, what I didn't appreciate as much, however, is that the skills that you develop in consulting are very relevant to the nonprofit world as well.

Interviewer: So was it just this one panel that got you interested?

The interviewer wants to be sure that the candidate didn't just have an isolated "Hallejulah consulting" moment.

Candidate: Since then, I've done more research on the industry by talking to classmates who are gung-ho on consulting and going to every consulting company's presentation. This has only solidified my interest in consulting: It will give me a really solid base of experience that I can use in whatever career I ultimately pursue.

Interviewer: Understood. Now let's talk about your internship last summer and how it prepared you for a life in consulting . . .

The candidate offers the interviewer a reasoned, logical explanation for why he wants to go into consulting. He will likely be tested on his analytic and quantitative skills through market-sizing and strategy cases, but at least he has "checked the box" on why he wants to go into consulting.

CASE 15

Objectively, as if you were answering on behalf of a colleague or supervisor at your former employer, tell me what you consider to be your biggest opportunity for development and improvement—the weak spot in your skill set as compared to your strengths.

This is really a question about BOTH strengths and weaknesses—which are always positioned as more palatable than an actual weakness. What this person is asking is not only what you need to improve to better round out your skill set for this role, but what you are doing about it. Let's face it—no one is a perfect, home-run match for any given role and the range of skills required to be successful in it. Everyone is relatively stronger in some areas and relatively weaker in others. What the interviewer wants here is an HONEST answer—not one that sounds so meticulously crafted as to be unbelievable or overly self-serving. The best answers here demonstrate that the candidate is self-aware and has listened and reacted to development feedback in prior roles. Solid job candidates will not only know what areas need improvement, they will also demonstrate a commitment to improvement.

Bad Answers

- I wouldn't say that anyone I used to work with or for would be able to tell you anything negative about my performance and skills. I really think they would all be nothing but complimentary about me and my work!

Not going to work—not only does it not ring true (everyone, even the most impressive business practitioners out there, has something to work on), but it indicates that the candidate is either too full of herself or fooling herself about how strong her skill set and work really are. A strong business practitioner actually pays attention in annual reviews and in feedback sessions and takes note of opportunities for improvement. A better approach is to consider the question, and answer it as honestly as you can—without completely undercutting yourself.

- Wow, that's really a hard one. You know, I feel like I'm strong at everything I do, but I can't really guess at what my old colleagues or boss might say. I'm really not sure . . . that's a hard one!

This kind of answer clearly communicates that the candidate hasn't interviewed much or hasn't prepared much, or both. This is a somewhat common resume question, and as such a good interviewer will have at least considered the prospect of a question like this and have a basic and adequate response considered (if not fully formed).

- I think that I'd have to say my weakest point is that I can be really hard to work with when I don't get my way. I tend to be really direct and adamant about my opinion on how to solve a problem when I know that I'm right, and other people sometimes find that hard to accept.

This would be an example of an answer that is either too honest or too severe to address the question without doing too much damage to your candidacy for the job. Furthermore, this is really a personal development opportunity for improvement, which may be true but which you aren't being asked to address in this interview. Stick to an answer that is both professional in nature and that doesn't reflect so negatively on you that it raises real red flags about your match to the job.

Good Answer

Candidate: Most recently, I worked as a business analyst for a management and systems consulting company. I'll tell you a piece of feedback about my work that I've taken seriously and taken to heart. I was told in my annual review that one of my biggest opportunities to improve as a business analyst is to complement my data collection by soliciting the perspectives and opinions of my colleagues who may know more about the industry or topic that I'm analyzing. I've learned that stepping back from the data and collaborating at least a little with more knowledgeable colleagues can usually help point out a piece of the analysis that the numbers don't always reveal.

The candidate does a good job of demonstrating that she listened in her reviews and feedback sessions, which is always a good sign, and that she wants to continue her development by improving in this area. In addition, the area she has chosen to highlight is certainly a prerequisite for a successful career in consulting—the ability to collaborate and step out of an "analysis silo" to make sure no obvious opportunities for the client are being missed. Finally, this answer rings true—it feels like it's probably true, and not just some feel-good answer that she invented before the interview so she had an answer to this question if it came up.

Candidate: I continue to work on making sure that I reach out to colleagues who might know more than I do when it's a relatively new topic area or business that I'm working on. Even though I am inclined to work hard and "go deep" on getting all the data I can when I face a new analytical problem, sometimes the past experience of someone else really helps me make up for a relative lack of experience in a new area.

The candidate is continuing on a good path here, connecting her knowledge of how improvement in this weak spot in the past will yield better results in the future.

Candidate: While I'm still getting better at this all the time, I really benefited from putting this into practice in the last project I worked on here in my business studies. I worked on a project with four other people analyzing a problem in the automotive industry. After I'd done an initial pass at running the numbers and doing some background research on the issue on the Internet, I asked my teammates over lunch one day if any of them knew much about car manufacturing that might be relevant to our project. It turned out that our quietest, most shy team member worked for a subsidiary of Ford when she was right out of college a few years back!

By asking that question, I was able to elicit some insights into the market forces that were giving rise to the business problem that our "client" in the case was facing—and all this was new information that she hadn't volunteered in our first few work sessions, probably because she didn't feel empowered to speak up! It was really helpful, and guided me to improve the data and information that we all used to complete our project and come to our conclusions. It was one time when I learned how helpful it could be when I worked to improve my analysis techniques and development in that regard. I'm still learning how to improve in this regard, but this was a time when I realized how helpful it can be to seek input from others.

The candidate remembered to come back to the question of what she could have done better, and she talks humbly but directly about the importance of improving in this area. This awareness—and connection of the problem area or weak spot in her skill set to the benefits she will realize as she continues to work on it—are valuable to any employer who wants an employee who can take direction and grow and improve on the job.

WETFEET'S INSIDER GUIDE SERIES

Job Search Guides

Getting Your Ideal Internship
Job Hunting A to Z: Landing the Job You Want
Killer Consulting Resumes!
Killer Cover Letters & Resumes!
Killer Investment Banking Resumes!
Negotiating Your Salary & Perks
Networking Works!

Interview Guides

Ace Your Case: Consulting Interviews
Ace Your Case II: 15 More Consulting Cases
Ace Your Case III: Practice Makes Perfect
Ace Your Case IV: The Latest & Greatest
Ace Your Case V: Return to the Case Interview
Ace Your Case VI: Mastering the Case Interview
Ace Your Interview!
Beat the Street: Investment Banking Interviews
Beat the Street II: I-Banking Interview Practice Guide

Career & Industry Guides

Careers in Accounting
Careers in Advertising & Public Relations
Careers in Asset Management & Retail Brokerage
Careers in Biotech & Pharmaceuticals
Careers in Brand Management
Careers in Consumer Products
Careers in Entertainment & Sports
Careers in Health Care
Careers in Human Resources
Careers in Information Technology
Careers in Investment Banking
Careers in Management Consulting

Careers in Marketing & Market Research
Careers in Nonprofits & Government Agencies
Careers in Real Estate
Careers in Retail
Careers in Sales
Careers in Supply Chain Management
Careers in Venture Capital
Industries & Careers for MBAs
Industries & Careers for Undergrads
Specialized Consulting Careers: Health Care, Human Resources, and Information Technology

Company Guides

25 Top Consulting Firms
25 Top Financial Services Firms
Accenture
Bain & Company
Booz Allen Hamilton
Boston Consulting Group
Credit Suisse First Boston
Deloitte Consulting
Deutsche Bank
The Goldman Sachs Group
J.P. Morgan Chase & Co.
McKinsey & Company
Merrill Lynch & Co.
Morgan Stanley
UBS

WetFeet in the City Guides

Job Hunting in New York City
Job Hunting in San Francisco